MEDITERRANEAN
C·O·L·O·R

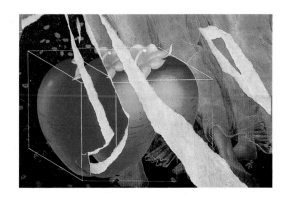

Photographs and Text by Jeffrey Becom

Foreword by Paul Goldberger

MEDITERRANEAN COLOR

Italy · France · Spain · Portugal · Morocco · Greece

ABBEVILLE PRESS   PUBLISHERS
NEW YORK   LONDON   PARIS

Contents

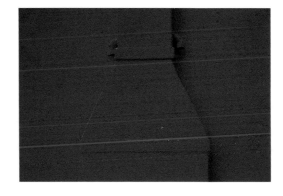

Foreword

Paul Goldberger

Jeffrey Becom's photographs are more brilliantly poised between abstraction and realism than any others I have ever seen. Or is it that they are poised between photography and painting? Or between the making of art and the documentation of architecture? Jeffrey Becom, like all important artists, has carved out his own territory, one that exists not above or beyond the territory we have seen before, but in the middle of it, in the interstices between the worlds that we already know. His photographs are abstract *and* realistic, at once; it is in the making of that balance, the finding of a world in between, that his art lies.

Jeffrey Becom has two missions: the documentation of a disappearing architectural culture and the creation of beautiful works of art. He is not the first photographer to have attempted to combine these often contradictory goals—it is hard not to think of Atget in Paris, or of Walker Evans in the United States—but he does it more freshly, more carefully, and finally more joyfully than any photographer in our time. The particular architectural culture of the brightly painted stucco vernacular of the Mediterranean countries that he has chosen to photograph would in anyone's hands, of course, yield different images from those of Atget or Evans; Jeffrey Becom's training as both a painter and an architect accentuates the differences still more. His photographs are lush, and they are vivid as a color-field painting; also like a painting, they deal in surface more than space. It is the walls that are the reality of the building to Jeffrey Becom, not the space within.

Yet his passion for the architectural thing itself, for the building and for the life that goes on within it, is everywhere apparent. These images are testaments to his love of where he goes and what he sees. The sheer richness of the photographs, in which color becomes a painterly presence, is enough to show us that. The color is what strikes the observer first: it is both intense and subtle, and printed so well that it becomes a sensuous thing in itself. The colors leap out at us, yet they are not at all intrusive; the perfection of the composition, the way in which these images seem so right within their frames, holds everything in check and brings a kind of restraint that the pigment itself does not always possess. Thus in *Blue Wall, Burano, Italy*

Painted Boats
Burano, Italy

(1982), the white-painted window frame near the top of the composition and the pale gray stones of the cornice combine to offset the intensity of the blue wall that fills the bulk of the frame. The balancing is more purely compositional in *Blue Steps, Kalymnos, Greece* (1987), in which steps, a door, and a stucco wall are all suffused with a blue that seems almost stage lighting and not paint.

So, too, do the textures of this architecture affect the image. Jeffrey Becom is photographing architecture of stucco and stone, washed with color; we feel the materials, their roughness and porousness, and the texture in the photographs mediates the intensity of the color, just as it does in reality. Thus we have an image such as *Green Surround, Tiznit, Morocco* (1987), in which the varying textures of the wall play off against the colors painted on them. The stucco wall shown in *Fresh Paint, Rhodes, Greece* (1987) is more even and consistent, and in a sense the joining of the wall itself to the rich salmon pink painted on it is all Becom is trying to shows us. But not entirely all: the way in which the salmon-pink field has been balanced with the green-painted square window opening and the green panel on the left shows us Jeffrey Becom's sensibility in a nutshell. Photography was never more an art of composition than here; but, for Becom, composing is narrowing down, focusing, knowing precisely where to crop the frame. He is not interested in great vistas or in huge swaths of buildings; we must look elsewhere for a sense of what these houses are like as complete objects, or for what kind of urban spaces these buildings make when they join together. He looks hard, bearing down, laserlike, at small snatches of façades, but then he raises them to magnificence.

We feel that especially in the occasional moments when Becom breaks away from purely vernacular architecture and turns his eye toward the monumental. Conveying magnificence is not so difficult a task when the subject is classical grandeur, but to do so through a tight, limited frame, in which only a small portion of a façade is visible, makes us see classicism with a new intensity. In images such as *Columns, Dolcedo, Italy* (1981) or *Candles, Volterra, Italy* (1981), the colors are the subtle colors of stone, the texture is rich and sensuous, but the real thing is the composition. Curiously, *Marble Pillars, San Marco, Venice* (1987), one of the only images of a well-known piece of architecture Becom has made, is one of the least successful—the skewed angle with which we see these great stone columns seems a bit forced, almost gimmicky beside the steady, straight-on views that Becom otherwise uses.

Becom is remarkably consistent. There are relatively few eccentric images here. Even in the rare occasions in which he departs from photographing buildings or parts of buildings, images such as *Fishing Boat, Tarhazoute, Morocco* (1987) or *Spice Seller's Wall, Essaouira, Morocco* (1987), the idea is the same: to take a tiny swath of the vernacular landscape and make of it a composition with the brilliance and intensity of an abstract painting. There are moments—and *Spice Seller's Wall* is one of them—when Becom's sensibility seems almost to resemble Joseph Cornell's. Here are tiny objects composed in such a way as to render them almost icons.

There are almost no people in these images, but unlike traditional architectural photography, in which people seem irrelevant, we sense here that they hover near, just outside of the frame. Much of this is due to the architecture itself. The sense always is of human scale and of human activity; a door, a window, a flowerpot on a sill, a religious icon, a clock. These images remind us more powerfully than any words can that clarity, simplicity, strength, and abstraction possess power and passion—and that they can be human values and not merely architectonic ones.

This is the book's most urgent message for architecture. In the last few years, as architects in developed societies have been seeking to break away from the austerity of orthodox modernism and restore a degree of sensuousness and emotion to architecture, this quest, which has come to be known as post-modernism, has been associated mainly with a return to ornament, decoration, and historical style. Indeed, there has been no small attempt made to make the association an automatic one between sensuousness in architecture and the revival of historic styles. Becom shows us that this need not be so, that these vernacular buildings, simple and plain yet lush, can match the emotional impact of any work of architecture.

He acknowledges these connections in his introduction, in which he speaks of the post-modern movement in architecture as having brought "a renewed interest in creating designs with cultural and historical associations and in using the symbolism of traditional forms, ornament, and color to return meaning to our built environment." All true, yet one would hardly want to think of our interest in these potent Mediterranean buildings as being but a by-product of post-modernism, which at its worst can be effete and cloying. One thinks, in contrast, of Le Corbusier's evocation of Mediterranean architecture as a prototype for modernism—although Le Corbusier loved Mediterranean buildings for their whiteness, while Becom sees their idiosyncratic and brilliant episodes of color.

That these vernacular buildings can be invoked by both modernists and post-modernists, even for somewhat opposite purposes, confirms their power as well as their glory; they are *hors concours* in the business of architectural debate. To a certain extent this is the nature of all vernacular architecture, of course; it is above the fray and has a kind of primal strength to it that can be read as meaning almost anything. There is no level of theoretical intent to these buildings; they just *are,* but their presence can tell us as much about a culture as do more consciously crafted works of architecture—sometimes more.

These images, one part Frankenthaler, one part Cornell, yet still completely and convincingly photography, can stand on their own without a single word. But the accompanying text removes all suspicion that Jeffrey Becom makes any pretense of being the objective recorder, documenting without comment; here he reveals to us a deep sensitivity for the Mediterranean cultures he is exploring, and no small degree of sophistication about the problems they face.

The old stucco houses and shopfronts of the Mediterranean, brightly washed with color, and the other moments in which color becomes a presence in Mediterranean architecture, are the ostensible subject of this book, and Becom reveals his love for them not only through the photographs but also through such passages in the text as his descriptions of the way homemade pigments are mixed in Burano. But the gradual arrival of the twentieth century and its effect on that culture is the hidden story that Jeffrey Becom also tells here. The images document and celebrate what has always been; the text explains how what has always been may no longer be. It is at times almost a kind of lament, laced not with sentimentality or with anger but with a dignified, measured sadness.

Becom's way of working is itself relevant to all of this. He does not swoop in by Concorde, dash through a town, and return with images held high like a trophy. Nor does he self-consciously and self-righteously take on the customs of the natives. Instead, he lingers and immerses himself; he moves slowly. He is not interested in imposing himself, but in viewing discreetly. He approaches with respect and deference and proceeds at the pace of the culture he is seeking to record and to celebrate. So process is important here—it is a part of this gentle artist's passion, a way in which he turns out to be true not only to the making of his art but to the values of his subject.

Becom's method is exact and deliberate, hardly like the Mediterranean cultures themselves. He is clearly happiest in those places in which he is left alone or can interact with people in his own way. But so comfortable is he with the sheer act of observing that he could have been a travel writer. And like many travel writers, the places that disturb him occasionally bring out his best writing. Of Morocco, he writes, "Moroccan merchants are entrepreneurial pit bulls. Merely walking past a shop invites attack." He goes on to say of his time there that "Daily existence becomes a comic opera of confusion, magic, beauty, and bewilderment," and, in a nice note of self-irony, concludes that in Morocco "Ambiguity is preferable to precision, and my programmed efficiency is not prized."

Here is Becom in Pisa, explaining how he avoids the tourist gauntlet surrounding the leaning tower: "I found that by walking from the train station through the quiet, arcaded streets of the lesser-known Pisa, I could avoid the vendors and arrive at the Field of Miracles through the back door." And when it comes to describing his arrival at the tower, he sees—as so few others have—that the truly startling thing is the lawn, not the leaning tower itself. Here Becom is not so much being contrary as being a good architecture critic, knowing that while the leaning tower does not, alas, rise above its hackneyed image, the composition of lawn, tower, and baptistery does.

His observations on Italian hill towns, those rugged and gentle presences on the landscape that in themselves epitomize all that Becom loves, show a welcome realism. Not for Jeffrey Becom are these places to be naively romanticized: "The isolation can be overwhelming and is especially cruel in winter, when villagers are imprisoned in cold stone houses. All year round there is that laborious hill to conquer before reaching fields, market, or home. To discontented youth, hill towns are more jail than refuge, but their understandable exodus drains the villages of vitality. And so, unfortunately, most hill towns seem destined to become ghost towns."

Becom recognizes, as too few photographers, architects, and painters do, that it is the life of these buildings, of these towns and villages, and not just their stones, that confers meaning upon them, and he knows that this life, quaint and pleasing as it may be to others, is not particularly easy to sustain at the end of the twentieth century. We will not lose the Italian hill towns or the Moroccan and the Portuguese and the Greek houses, but we may well lose the life that goes on within them. The rough stones will remain, but the streets will become quieter, the piazzas emptier, and the glorious colors will finally fade, living still only in Jeffrey Becom's photographs.

For the Colors

The houses of farmers and fishermen in the lands bordering the Mediterranean Sea have been my focus for the past ten years. These simple shelters, and particularly the variety and beauty of the colors with which they are painted, fascinate me for the history and traditions they reveal. Even more, the façades offer me subject and palette from which to derive my own work as I, in turn, document their naive brilliance.

For well over a thousand years the monumental architecture of Europe's cathedrals, halls, and palaces has adapted to reflect successive fashions and favored styles, from the simplicity of early Romanesque to excessively elaborate rococo, with little concern for time, cost of labor, or extravagance of materials. In contrast, the peasant houses of the Mediterranean region, following only the framework of tradition, have changed little through the years. Neither pretentious, heroic, nor esoteric, these basic homes were built efficiently by anonymous craftsmen with limited skills and resources to overcome fundamental problems of survival.

Malarial lowlands and marauding invaders forced many of the Mediterranean's early inhabitants to steep, rocky terrain. The sheer effort of building on difficult sites demanded the simplest of designs. Harsh summers and cold winters dictated small windows and doorways. These were set within thick walls formed from the abundant stone, clay, and sand, with wood from scarce forests reserved for doors and roof supports. People found what worked for their practical needs. Tradition passed on their ingenious solutions. Communities formed; and the small, unassuming houses, when combined into villages, often became extraordinarily dramatic, as in the fortified hill towns of Spain and Italy. But still the individual house was usually a tiny, squarish structure of little character or distinction.

Painting, which was required on a regular basis to protect the stuccoed rubblestone or mud-brick walls and the wooden door and window frames, presented the resident with an immediate and affordable way of expressing individuality, identity, and pride. When enlivened by a unique coat of untutored colors, these humble, centuries-old dwellings became a special product of the owner's creative personality. Rich

Mud Wall
Assaka, Morocco

colors and fanciful designs drew attention away from life's sameness and concealed the surrounding poverty. At the same time, the annual selection of tints provided a small opportunity for control in a world otherwise ruled by Church and nature.

Modernist architects earlier in this century tended to dismiss their Western architectural heritage, eliminating traditional forms, applied decoration, and, on the whole, a sense of place in favor of "international" buildings evoking modern industrial life. They emphasized forms based solely on function, rather than historical precedent, and the "honest" use of unadulterated materials such as unfinished concrete and unpainted wood and steel. With few exceptions, vernacular architecture was ignored or condemned as the antithesis of the machine age.

With today's post-modern movement in architecture and design comes a looking backward to both monumental and vernacular patterns and a revival of past styles. There is renewed interest in creating designs with cultural and historical associations and in using the symbolism of traditional forms, ornament, and color to return meaning to our built environment. This has catapulted the common man's *architettura spontanea* from relative obscurity to academic scrutiny, professional respect, and wider appreciation. Traditional architecture is being reordered and reworked, borrowed from, mocked, and played with in wild new combinations. Painted color is again seen as a way of accentuating form or camouflaging the consequences of a meager budget's prohibition of ornament or fine materials, just as a Greek fisherman has always highlighted his front door surround bold blue or a Portuguese farmer might false marble his house façade.

Monumental architecture of the Mediterranean countries has been thoroughly documented and can be readily studied. Because of their unanimously acknowledged stature and obvious value from tourism, these buildings are in little danger of disappearing. Living vernacular architecture, however, is an endangered species.

In northern Europe, World War II wiped out large areas. Development has all but eliminated the remnants of traditional life. Indigenous buildings have been relegated to a few overly restored tourist centers or exiled to the artifice of open-air museums, and heirs of the builders, reduced to mere spectators or caretakers.

Traditional life is more persistent in southern Europe. But even in my brief decade of working in this region, I have seen foreboding signs. Without a doubt the most common disaster to befall vernacular architecture is the migration of the young people. They leave their villages to study, or to work in the industrial North, while the old and infirm remain to watch their half-deserted towns crumble about them. Tourism has come to dominate the livelihood of many of the more photogenic Mediterranean towns. These communities generally capitalize on their popularity by commercializing traditional life until it fades into a parody of itself. Customs atrophy. Religious ceremonies derail into marketing ploys. The tools and trappings of popular life are translated into fashion accessories and sold in the souvenir shops that have usurped ingenuous houses. Soon concrete doubles for stone, asphalt supplants cobblestone, and aluminum windows and steel doors replace wood.

With this climb into the twentieth century, life arguably becomes more comfortable and convenient but slowly loses touch with the past. And as values change, the buildings do as well. Traditional color, detail, and embellishment disappear first, followed by the houses themselves. Through my photography I attempt to celebrate the beauty that remains in these faded stucco walls. I react to, rather than direct or manipulate my subjects, taking care that my images retain a strong association with the culture and location within which they exist rather than becoming idealized, abstract color compositions.

Although there are many fine books concentrating on the native architecture of the Mediterranean, they contain virtually no mention of the colloquial use of color. I dedicate this book to these remarkable colors. I believe they constitute a vast treasury of references bearing on the origins, derivations, and applications of color in Western architecture, which directly reverberate through today's design.

Mediterranean Color represents my personal record of time spent observing, studying, and photographing the anonymous architecture of the region between 1978 and 1988. Occasionally, in these pilgrimages, my eye has been captured by other colorful man-made subjects, such as painted boats and street shrines, or by elements of buildings of "higher" architectural status. Some of these images are included here as well. I have also often strayed far beyond the shores of the Mediterranean Sea, into Portugal and down the Atlantic coast of Morocco. Yet incorporating these regions is grounded in a common history and shared spirit.

I recognize that the photographs are not evenly distributed, nor are they impartially balanced throughout the region. After so much time spent looking, I have naturally found special, cherished places that lure me year after year. While I have devotedly combed small areas that hold the colors that intrigue me, such as Burano, Italy, and southern Portugal, some Mediterranean countries are underrepresented or missing entirely. Many cultures either do not contain or perpetuate the combination of color, tradition, and architecture to which I am drawn. My prejudice for small, quiet villages with eccentric histories and archaic customs narrows my map even further. But the absent lands also disclose that I have not exhausted the area's potential. There are many places I hope one day to discover as I continue my search.

Some of my knowledge of these lands has been gleaned from guidebooks and the writings of other travelers. But my text is mostly derived from my own journals of impressions and random conversations with the people who live in the houses, work in the buildings, and sail in the boats. Relying on a jumble of foreign vocabularies in an attempt to find a common though limited language, we share histories; and I

Farmhouse
Vale de Judeu, Portugal

gather stories of the villagers' lives, legends, homes, and customs from whomever seems eager to talk. While I've certainly missed some explanations and lost others in translation, I have tried to substantiate the folktales and building lore whenever possible. To close the gaps, however, I have sometimes made inductive leaps.

Anonymous buildings do not allow the same kind of strict historical research as monumental architecture. But their investigation can return a reward richer in relevant insights than study of a great cathedral and its treasures. Interpreting the workings of a humble village and its painted houses grants me a deeper understanding of the everyday life the majority of people have lived throughout history. And this is more pertinent to me than insights into the lives and luxuries of kings and popes.

I come to my theme through a logical progression. Born in Shelbyville, Indiana, in 1953, I have painted since I was twelve years old. My earliest subjects were neighboring barns and silos. During high school I studied printmaking and hardline abstract color composition under the direction of a transplanted Austrian artist who had settled in my hometown.

In 1971 I started to take the camera seriously and experimented with both black-and-white and color darkroom techniques. That same year I entered the University of Cincinnati's College of Design, Art, and Architecture. My education was grounded in the modernist theories of the Bauhaus, which stressed conceptual design and encouraged interdisciplinary study. But to avoid contamination from past styles, my training was severely limited with regard to art and architectural history. On my first trip to Europe in 1976 with two fellow architecture students, I discovered a world of monumental and vernacular buildings I had missed.

Following six years in the program at Cincinnati, which balanced classes with work in architectural offices, I received my degree in architecture. To escape the Midwest's winters and investigate West Coast design, I moved to San Francisco to practice. After designing and overseeing construction of an unconventional Telegraph Hill residence, I abandoned the frustrations and limitations of the business of architecture to channel all my energy toward painting and photography.

I began to divide my time between work in my Berkeley studio and annual travels abroad. I first studied Gothic cathedrals at Amiens and then at Chartres, with historian Malcolm Miller, in an effort to begin filling the gaps in my knowledge of architectural history. At home, I completed restoration of my 1920s bungalow, produced eccentric furniture and clocks, and slowly progressed on a twelve-panel icon in oil and gold and silver leaf on wood, summing up my cathedral studies. As a painter, however, my attention was gradually wooed away from architectural landmarks by the colors of small, anonymous houses in isolated Italian hill towns.

Watercolor travels easily, so it became the medium I used to capture these hues and simple architectural elements. I developed a drybrush technique, which allowed me to render the detail as well as the color when painting on site. My work in architecture had taught me that the best way to describe something is in a very straightforward manner, as with a plan or elevation. In my painting I took the same approach. Once in a long while I would find subjects in which the subtlety and richness of the colors were already so perfect to me that to paint them seemed futile. These I photographed instead, and so began my Wall Series.

Today, between painting and preparing photographs for exhibition, I continue the discovery process overseas. Without forethought of a book to catalog the project, I have proceeded with this private obsession at my own pace, following weather, currency exchange rates, train schedules, and legends rather than a fixed itinerary. Admittedly my choices are more often fortunate or impulsive than systematic and scholarly. I get waylaid a lot. I make no reservations and travel with an open-ended return. Basing myself in one place for many weeks, I move constantly within that area, scouring every tiny crossroads for prospective images. Decisions are made from day to day and hour to hour, as very few places fulfill the promise of the color I am after, and I must move on.

Living modestly, I sleep in small *pensioni* and eat out of farmers' markets and *tavernas.* I have slept on the beach when the inevitable unexpected crush of a local festival meant no rooms were available, and I have stayed in four-star hotels when prices permitted. Larger cities are useful for restocking supplies, attending to laundry, obtaining a visa, and enjoying more complex meals or a genuine hotel for a few nights. Nice and Florence each have a photo shop I have come to depend on for fresh film and camera repair. I often make runs to the French or Swiss border from the tip of southern Italy or Spain to entrust my undeveloped film to a reliable postal service for shipment home. Cities always have good bookstores and libraries, too, for gathering more detailed information about an area that holds potential, and they are usually the only efficient embarcation points for the most remote villages.

I rely on buses and trains for long distances; but whether returning to favorite sites or surveying new locations, I mostly walk, up to ten and twelve hours a day. Speed breeds urgency. I have found that having a car sets the pace of a journey, and its convenience and comfort often make getting out to see something on slow inspection much less likely. Exploring on foot allows me to immerse myself in the life and architecture until I finally begin to know my surroundings and see the things generally overlooked by motorized travelers.

My sort of photographic expedition requires that I travel light. Keeping my equipment to a minimum in both weight and size allows me to walk the long distances to and through the reclusive villages where my photographs are found. I have pared down to one camera, a Nikon F3; one lens, a 35mm Nikkor perspective control; and one film, Kodachrome 64. I no longer carry a tripod. In addition, I have chosen a single color process, Cibachrome, which lets me make archivally stable, direct-positive color prints from my transparencies. Although I no longer produce all the prints myself, all photographs are hand-printed and processed under my direct supervision.

A lifetime of disciplining my eyes and thirteen years' experience understanding Cibachrome's advantages and limitations allow me to eliminate or determine before the photograph is taken many of the usual decisions related to the final print. To compensate for inherently contrasty Kodachrome and Cibachrome materials, for example, I deliberately avoid strong light, working instead on cloudy or rainy days, or returning at dusk to the façades I have been most struck by during the day's wanderings. Thus, by simultaneously limiting as many variables as possible, including my subject and the way I approach it, I have been able both to control and subordinate most technical considerations. This frees me to concentrate on seeing.

Because of the strict bounds of my inquiry, my images ordinarily do not include people or landscape. This is intentional. It does not mean that I have no interest in or compassion for the land and the people with whom I surround myself for so many months each year. But to portray these effectively would require a separate commitment. As it is, I will often take two thousand photographs in the course of a single trip. Upon my return I select fewer than one hundred for darkroom consideration and will print twenty-five. Of these, sometimes five will remain as permanent images in my gallery portfolio, representing the five to six months of concentrated effort.

Out of my interest in vernacular architecture arose my fascination with places and objects of devotion. These weathered shrines, miracle-working madonnas, good-luck charms, and votive offerings are closely linked to daily life in the most traditional villages. I find these representations of faith marvelous and bewildering, coming as I do from computer-generated America and my own Protestant upbringing. That an Italian widow dedicates hours each day to kneeling before the statue of a saint, or a Spanish father commissions a *retablo* for the church when his son is restored to health, that a Moroccan bus stops at prayer time so passengers may prostrate themselves by the side of the road, or a Greek fisherman finds solace in the silver *tamata* he has hung in his boat for safety: these seeming anachronisms, hand in hand with traditions of color, are keys to the motivations and values of very complex and ritual-bound peoples.

These vestiges of something lost and mysterious are not easy for me to decipher. The people I meet are confused by my values as well. Often it is difficult to explain why I am standing with my back to their most noted monument or panorama, photographing a crumbling wall. So, among the first words I learn and use in each Mediterranean language are: *per i colori, pelas cores, yia ta chromata, porque dellas tintas, pour ses couleurs.* For the colors.

THE MEDITERRANEAN

France

Santiago de Compostela•

Santillana del Mar•

Carcassonne•

MARSEILLE

Póvoa de Varzim•
Vila do Conde•
Espinho•   •PORTO
Murtosa•
Costa Nova•

BARCELONA

Portugal

•MADRID

Spain

Obidos•

Cruz de Pedra• •LISBON

•Estremoz

M E D I

Lagos•
Silves•
Vale de Judeu•   •Faro
Purgatório•
Loule•

•SEVILLE

•GRANADA

•Almería

M E D I

GIBRALTAR

ATLANTIC OCEAN

Asilah•

•Chaouen

•RABAT   •FES

•CASABLANCA

Morocco

Algeria

Essaouira•   •MARRAKESH

Tarhazoute•
Agadir•   •Taroudannt
           •Hafaya

Tiznit• •Assaka
         •Tafraoute

Italy

Italians love excess. This is revealed in every aspect of their operatic lives: big voices and gestures, incredibly late trains, an exaggerated sense of honor and pride, voluptuously extended meals, and the lira with its millions of zeros. Every dispute is a war and each meeting a reunion. And all descriptions are unhesitatingly heightened to superlatives. Italians also adore excess in their architecture and will fawn over the most ornately contrived baroque extravagances and outlandish gilded plaster doodles. This affection shows, too, in their use of color.

Color is at the heart of Italy and always has been, from the ancient frescoes of Pompeii to the latest Milanese designs in furniture and fashion, from the bustling port of Trieste to the street processions of Naples. But nowhere is this color more apparent than in her buildings. Yellow ocher and blood red, pale pink, peach, and apricot, sunburnt cinnamon and sienna, deep turquoise and olive green, ultramarine, burgundy, and bronze: these are the colors of earth and sea and sun and sky. They are the lusty colors of ripe fruit and wine, of chaotic outdoor markets, fervent church rites, and public arguments. The colors of art and empire. The colors of life.

It was Italy's colors that first defined my goal and set me on the road. I still spend a large part of every journey here. The areas that entice me most are each so individual as to seem separate countries: the Venetian Lagoon with its brightly

Pink Wall
Monterosso, Italy

Painted Walls
Burano, Italy

painted island houses washed in fog; the Riviera of pastel cliff-wedged villages and green terraced vineyards stepping to the sea; central Italy's cypress and wheat and somber fortified hill towns of varicolored stone; and the South, hot and dry, with cave towns and *trulli* houses splashed with color, twisted olive and vine, witches, and roadside shrines. Throughout, whether in traditional or innovative ways, Italians use color more often, more lavishly, and more passionately than any other Mediterranean people.

Venice's story begins in her lagoon, for the islands of this great salt lake are the source of her earliest people and riches. As the Roman Empire fell into ruin in the fifth century, Visigoths and then Huns penetrated northern Italy. The terrified populace took flight toward their only escape, the sea, where horse-bound invaders could not follow through the marshy waters. The lagoon's islands offered safe retreat for these refugees, who escaped with little more than their most valued possessions, the relics from their churches.

The first settlers spun wool as had their mainland ancestors. They soon learned to farm by securing the shifting soil with mats of woven rushes. But the sea held greater promise. First from fishing and salt gathering, eventually through shipbuilding and the trade of salt for spices from the East, they accumulated vast wealth. Great cities rose, but fell as persistent barbarians sacked islands still accessible from the mainland, and as the tide retreated from the outer lagoon, bringing stagnant water and malaria. In the eighth century the far-flung inhabitants congregated on a group of islets in the center of the lagoon, where health and safety were assured. And so Venice began. Some of the original islands were completely abandoned and others transformed into places of prayer. But many nodded into the drowsy fishing communities they remain today. One of these, Burano, is my prize, the most colorful square mile in the entire Mediterranean.

Away from Venice, beyond melancholy San Michele, the cemetery isle, where women wrapped in black carry bundles of gladioli; past Murano, the isle of glass with its pristine Byzantine church and hideous crystal bric-a-brac; and deep in the silent, mist-covered lagoon lies the tiny, secluded island of Burano. There is nothing monumental here. The land barely rises above the level of the sea, and only an ancient, leaning *campanile* breaks the skyline. Canals cut through the green meadows surrounding Burano's one small village, whose occcupants have fished and made lace through the centuries.

Sounds are muffled in the fog. Cries of seabirds and fishmongers, boats creaking at their stays, the occasional accordion melody or opera record filtered through a doorway, and the heavy, gray water lapping at the sides of the canals seem distant, dreamlike, and supernaturally soft compared to the crush of Venice an hour away.

In startling opposition to this pervasive calm is the island's use of color, which ranges from rich and harmonious to gaudy and shocking. Seemingly every possible combination of hue, tone, pattern, and texture is represented on the houses and the boats. Inexplicably, such predominance of radiant color is unique to Burano in this part of the Mediterranean. Until recently the shades were more subdued, with pigments derived from the nearby Italian earth. In the past fifty years, however, this tradition has been supplemented by brilliant imported pigments, although most of the paint is still handmade by the islanders.

The homemade paint is a mixture of powdered lime, salt water, and glue to which are added various ground colors. When dry, this paint is highly absorbent and readily soaks in the lagoon's moist climate and salt air. Coupled with the fugitive nature of some of the lower-quality pigments, fading, peeling, mottling, and a continuous need to repaint result. Many residents use this as an opportunity to change colors and combinations annually. They take obvious pride in and pleasure from this exaggerated tradition of painting; so, fortunately, it seems destined to continue.

On a recent visit to Burano with my wife, Sally, I delivered a print to the owner of one of the houses I had photographed five years earlier. It was a completely different composition of colors than when I had seen it last. After accepting the picture and smiling over the changes his house had undergone, the man returned to his task at hand—whitewashing, as an undercoat for the year's new set of hues. By the end of the day, the formerly royal-blue and maroon, then lobster-red and yolk-yellow fisherman's cottage was vermilion and shocking pink.

Burano life is set against this constantly changing collage of vibrant façades lining the canals. Outside these walls, near open doorways dressed with equally flamboyant colored cloth, preside the fishermen's wives. Many sit on tiny, fire-engine red, cane-seated chairs, tending small charcoal fires grilling the midday meal or tying lace, so often a companion of nets. While they work, they share their front steps with great barrels of wriggling black eels, brought by their men who row past them a few feet away, in boats painted as boldly as their houses.

Fresh paint brushed frequently and generously on a simple fishing boat transforms it from a commonplace vessel into a uniquely personal possession. And while lively colors will not assure success, the Burano fisherman may have found that they make him feel a bit better about a bad day's catch.

By midafternoon, when the mist has lifted, Burano starts to steam, and walking becomes impossible. I then take the boat to even more secluded Torcello for a picnic among the scattered stones and monuments. Now just a few families, some ruins,

Wall with Deck Chair
Burano, Italy

Blue Wall
Burano, Italy

Red Chair
Burano, Italy

and a small cluster of Byzantine buildings remain at the end of the *vaporetto* line as the only reminder of the glories of the first great city of the Venetian Lagoon. Nothing breaks the calm, and except for occasional students of art or lost tourists, the island is deserted. I sit alone in the grassy main square among a jumble of carved stone, my lunch of cherries, sardines, and biscuits resting on the remnant of a column capital. In the still, tideless water, reflection often outdoes reality. The sky turns to burnished silver, shadows to jet black, and crumbling colored walls and untended painted boats become beautiful abstract patterns.

As dusk approaches I return to Burano to photograph. On warm summer evenings the island's entire population joins in *passeggiata*, strolling in twos and threes, arm in arm under the dim, yellow streetlamps. Whole families together circle the main square, pushing baby strollers over the flagstones past the cathedral and the lace school, eating *gelati*, and stopping to talk with their neighbors, shopkeepers, and café owners.

"It's a good life here," the eighty-nine-year-old woman standing beside her fluorescent-blue house tells me. "The fishing is good, the water is fine for the children to swim, it is quiet and small, I know everyone. I'm happy here." This serene contentment is contagious. I feel it each time I visit.

After *passeggiata* I catch the last boat back to Venice. It is night, and the lights from the *vaporetto* are the only thing that can be seen in the dark lagoon. Mosquitoes are attracted from all around. Soon every passenger is engaged in battle, flailing and squashing the bugs on arms and windows. Finally, the beleaguered captain turns out all but the running lights; and we proceed slowly toward Venice in eerie darkness.

I will never forget my first sight of Venice. I had taken the night train from Paris. We rolled past vestiges of the Venetian Republic, the winged lions and pointed arches of Vicenza, Verona, and Padua. With dawn the train approached the lagoon. Water and sky merged in a gray mist cut by a silver ribbon of track vanishing into the distance. The sky turned pink and the water platinum. Fishing nets, supported on twisted sticks, stretched across the shallow marsh. Alongside the train slid a thin black boat, two standing oarsmen rhythmically keeping pace.

The train slowed into the modern, nondescript station, breaking my trance. Under the big clocks, well-dressed businessmen, grandmothers in black, and loudly clad tourists bristling with cameras mixed on the platform. I passed through the knot of students sprawled on the exit stairs and, suddenly, centuries fell away.

Gallina
Verona, Italy

Before me lay the palaces of the Grand Canal, faded rose and gold and peach and cream, with bulbous domes, flamelike arches, classical pediments, and stones from every corner of the ancient world embedded in their walls. Alabaster and ophite, porphyry and jasper, and an infinite variety of colored and patterned marbles carved with Byzantine peacocks, pomegranates, and griffins, Chinese merchants, pagan deities, the Virgin Mary, and the Islamic eye of God, all joined to form a rich, exotic, incongruous assemblage.

I walked contentedly for hours, crossing low-stepped bridges at every turn. Gondolas passed below me, twisting in the flashing black water. Deeper into the Venetian labyrinth I roamed, intentionally lost, with no thought of learning where I was or where I had been. Occasionally I would recognize landmarks, towers and domes appearing, disappearing, and seeming to stray, as I navigated the narrow lanes. Here, free from the car exhaust and constant roar of motorcycles that fill the rest of Italy, the sounds and smells of Venice filtered down from hidden sources. I could hear someone singing, women calling from window to window, and a radio tuned to soccer. I tasted salt in the air and smelled the sea mingled with baking bread. And then, unexpectedly, I came upon Piazza San Marco.

These first impressions have been sharpened by many visits into an understanding that Venice holds two worlds. There is the city of marble, awe-inspiring and theatrical, its purpose long past. And the less-seen village of brick and stucco, where life today resides in peaceful courtyards and small cafés, at oratories and behind closed passageways. The two are intertwined. But aided by new, well-meaning signs, which point the most direct path to the Rialto Bridge and Saint Mark's, visitors are now much less apt to become lost and discover the other Venice, the village in the midst of monuments.

Venice straddles ninety-eight tiny islets, each one built on a similar plan. In the center is an open square paved in stone, bare except for the public well and a few benches. Fronting this *campo* is the church, holding relics of the beloved neighborhood saint. Once-grand houses surround the square. In varying states of deterioration, they endure: cold and damp most of the year, lacking adequate plumbing, their balconies hung with flowerpots and caged birds for want of gardens. Such homes, together with an economy that offers only jobs as servants to the tourist trade, have chased young Venetians to the mainland in search of more fulfilling work and less romantic but more comfortable quarters. And so, in what was once the most densely populated city in Europe, fewer than one hundred thousand people remain, mostly the old and the poor with nowhere else to go.

Venice is built on legends. Among the first tells of the villagers of Padua who sought direction from Heaven to escape Attila's onslaught. They were rewarded

Ex-Votos
Venice, Italy

Tapestry Boat
Venice, Italy

when pigeons, with tiny crosses over their heads and fledglings in their beaks, led them to a group of islets in the center of the nearby lagoon. Because the place where the birds landed was slightly elevated, they called the spot *Rivo Alto* (high embankment), the future site of the Rialto Bridge and the center of Venice. The pigeons infesting Piazza San Marco today are said to be descendants of these celestial guides.

For several centuries Venice remained a small, isolated fishing village. But when islanders of the outer lagoon joined together to form a city here, she grew and prospered. By the ninth century the Venetians, who had been far more concerned with material than spiritual rewards, had not found time to develop a local saint of sufficient merit to match their increasing financial and political importance. And so they stole one.

Sanctioned by a dream in which Saint Mark begged rescue from the land of infidels, two Venetian sailors snatched his remains from a shrine in Alexandria, Egypt, where he was also revered. They stuffed his bones in a barrel of salt pork, guaranteed to discourage Moslem search, and spirited them back to their city. The whimsical clergy justified the theft by fabricating a legend of their own. They announced that a shipwrecked Saint Mark had once been stranded on the future site of Venice, where, he was told by God, his body would one day rest in the most beautiful city in the world.

The people of Venice immediately began erecting a suitable home for their treasured relics. Since the city rests on sand and mud and all building materials must be imported, a glorious six-hundred-year scavenger hunt commenced for the best that could be purchased or pillaged. The crumbling palaces of the abandoned upper lagoon were quarried first. Then, all sea captains were required by law to return with something superb to adorn the basilica. Later, Crusaders looted Christian Constantinople and made off with more precious materials, for which the Venetian Republic was promptly excommunicated. No fine stone or statue was safe; and Saint Mark's, with its roving bones, became a vast, jeweled reliquary, a mosaic of marble and gold.

Ironically, it was the young Venetian Marco Polo—whose opening of the Orient brought Venice even greater wealth and power—who precipitated her downfall. His thirteenth-century tales of adventure and fortune in far-off lands inspired other great explorers, including Portugal's Vasco da Gama, who discovered an African Cape passage to India. This new sea route broke Venice's trading monopoly and sent her into a slow and extravagant decline. Buildings, art, and life became ever more excessive and elaborate as Venetians struggled to retain their image in the face of fading glory. *Carnevale* lost its religious ties and mutated into a six-month orgy of

Marble Pillars
San Marco, Venice, Italy

self-indulgence. Trees that shaded the piazzas were ripped out to make room for lavish tournaments, bullfights, and pig races. And all of Venice was a riot of color.

Frescoes, painted by the likes of Tintoretto and Titian, were emblazoned on many palaces. The citizens of Venice dressed in Eastern silk and turbans of brilliant colors. Ten thousand pink, violet, and chartreuse gondolas with gilt prows, Oriental carpets, and deep burgundy and green velvet canopies crowded the canals. But moisture from the lagoon claimed the frescoes. Fashions changed as Venice lost her hold on the Orient. And in the sixteenth century a law decreed that all gondolas be painted black to curb ostentation and commemorate a virulent outbreak of the plague.

One year I spent several weeks weaving along both sides of the Grand Canal, dodging pigeons and motor-boat wakes while studying and photographing the faded, decaying palaces that line the waterway. A succession of hot, oppressively humid days made my movements slow and deliberate. Finally, one afternoon the weather broke dramatically. A strong, cold wind began blowing from the north, followed by a solid bank of storm clouds.

I took cover with the old men in a café fronting a canal near the Rialto Bridge. On a low stone wall outside was the not-so-thriving enterprise of a small, thin, middle-aged man wearing the ubiquitous straw hat and striped shirt of a gondolier. I had seen him slumped there each day, lethargically trying to convince passing tourists to buy his plug-in, light-up plastic gondolas from a delicately balanced pyramidal display. Now he was standing for the first time in my memory, staring up at the rolling black clouds.

Suddenly it began to hail, and he was startled into action as wind sent his merchandise sailing into the canal: miniature gondolas of all sizes, bobbing and sinking in the choppy water. Many souvenirs were lost that day. The pensioners and I tried to help him save his remaining goods, but little could be done before we all had to run for shelter as lightning and rain intensified. The vendor, wringing his hands, was little consoled by wine and talk. The next day I passed the gondola salesman again. He was set up in his usual spot, depressed and down on inventory, but reassured—his Italian fatalism fully confirmed.

Italy's Riviera, stretching eastward from the border of southern France past Genoa to La Spezia, could boast of some of the most beautiful shoreline in the entire Mediterranean if it had either the energy or the inclination. Low mountains rise directly from the sea, and compact villages of pastel houses cling to the cliffs. I return often to this string of tiny, unself-conscious

port towns with their half-hearted beach trappings. Unlike the cosmopolitan chic of the nearby French Riviera, where traditional life and architecture have been bent or uprooted to accommodate the tanning of the rich and famous, these Italian counterparts in the sun have retained the integrity of their customs and painted colors.

The most dramatic of all these coastal communities are the Cinqueterre (Five Lands): Monterosso, Vernazza, Corniglia, Manarola, and Riomaggiore. Climbing terraced hills bright green with vineyards, the five villages nestle between adjoining promontories sheltering miniature bays. The fishermen here whose towns have no port must still drag their boats to safety each evening up steep ramps cut from the living rock.

Blush pinks, worn blues, and soft shades of melon green and amber linger in the stuccoed walls of houses and shops surrounding black-and-white-striped marble churches. On checkered stone piazzas, village life thrives. Women snap beans or knit while children ride tricycles and play soccer, dodging dripping laundry overhead. Old men have dragged wooden chairs away from cafés, just to the edge of acceptable loan. Thus ensconced, the elders readily give unsolicited advice to the fishermen repairing their boats or nets. And they shout lusty greetings to the young men with sickles and baskets, passing through from work in the vineyards, who line up to wash in the cold water of old stone fountains.

These daily routines are temporarily interrupted each summer by a rush of Italian tourists. Only then are the brightly painted boats relegated to the far ends of beaches so that these solo-phobics can squeeze against one another on the tiny sand and pebble coves. Italians seem not to exist except in groups, especially on holiday, when they all go to the same spot at the same time while, a mile away, peace and isolation reign.

The Cinqueterre are showing the first effects of supplemental income from the visitors, whose numbers swell each year. Old wooden doors and windows are displaced by gold-tone aluminum. The characteristic clay-tiled roofs are giving way to concrete slabs and corrugated sheet metal as rooms to let are plopped on. But additional money also means that paint is now being applied far more frequently, and it is a pleasure to see small villages so alive and fresh with color. My *Pink Wall* photograph was taken in Monterosso while the tiny home was still wet from the owner's brush. When I next saw the house, the façade had lost its sheen. Partially obscured by a gaudy pair of striped pajamas waving ceremoniously from a balcony overhead, the yellow scalloped eaves had paled to cream. It was time to paint again.

Rome has only recently cut roads through this rugged terrain. The rail line took decades to complete and now consists of endless tunnels punctuated by momentary flashes of villages and sea below. A short trip between two villages by train becomes

Ladder
Corniglia, Italy

hours of strenuous hiking on the steep, stony mule trail, which for former generations was the only link by land to their four nearest neighbors and the outside world. This snaking path zigzags along mountain ridges and through vineyards, past cascades, over streams, and beside little shrines marked with wildflowers and flickering votive candles.

Once, while walking along the trail between Monterosso and Vernazza, Sally and I came upon a local official sleeping soundly on a stone bench carved from the cliff face. Beside him lay his open briefcase full of papers. All around spread a spectacular, sweeping view. He had found the perfect office.

Up the coast from the Cinqueterre is Camogli, its name a contraction of *casa moglie* (wives' houses), which describes a painting tradition begun by its women. Left alone all day while their men fished, they dressed their narrow, six-story houses in striking colors, so that each man could recognize his home from sea. Time and weather have mellowed the once showy shades to tints of pink, ivory, and ocher.

As in many towns along the Riviera, most notably Varigotti and Sestri Levante, the buildings of Camogli are often frescoed in order to appear more impressive. Counterfeit divisions of large, rusticated stone, forged pediments and statuary, and simulated windows, shutters, and shrines emerge from the plain, flat plaster walls in glorious three-dimensional relief. This is *scagliuola,* a transfiguring process by which gypsum, pigment, and glue form images more flamboyantly elaborate than gravity or the pocketbook could ever allow. As time wears on these cosmetics, however, they begin to crack, peel, and run, with odd results. Suddenly half a window disappears, or what seems at a distance to be heavy stonework flecks and curls, giving away the secret.

In addition to these coastal towns, I have visited literally hundreds of dots on the map in the adjacent interior. Disregarded by guidebooks and tourists, these forgotten villages are poorer than their seaside neighbors. Life moves at a slower, more contemplative pace. The closely spaced *frazioni,* each occupied now by only a few extended families, sit on hills covered with forests of chestnut, beech, and pine. Walking between them is much easier than trying to locate the bus, which runs on an indecipherable and often illegible schedule mysteriously tuned to a calendar of markets, festivals, and crops.

From Apricale, with house piled upon house forming tunnellike passageways, to the tattered medieval walls of Zuccarello, with its river flowing past one long, double-arcaded street, these diminished towns of peeling frescoes and faded paint are each quite distinct from one another but for their churches. A gifted salesman of baroque designs must have moved through this region centuries ago, declaiming the rewards and virtues of raising such edifices. Now every little community has

Wall with Handprint
Varigotti, Italy

Columns
Dolcedo, Italy

Green Door
Apricale, Italy

inherited a vast baroque cathedral of cracked gilded plaster, weathered stone, and brick. Undulating entrances squirm with *putti,* pilasters, and pillars. Life-size saints appear to wriggle from niches, as if to evade eternal duty on the ledges. Within, occasional worshipers gather in small side chapels, abandoning the rest of the uncomfortably large space to dust and mildew.

Inland, visitors are few; and since I stay awhile, I am a rarity. Villagers stop to ask where I am from and if I know their cousin in Chicago or New York. They always offer their homemade wine and urge me to stay for the noonday meal of pasta and perhaps the chicken pecking at my feet. Overjoyed by the possibility that a photo can be made and mailed back to them on my return home, the men stand with their shirt sleeves rolled up, arms over one another's shoulders, while the women proudly display their overweight children. There is a moment of *adagio* when I signal that the shutter is ready to snap. Everyone suddenly stands perfectly still, wide-eyed, stiff, and smileless, posing for their record, unsure of the workings of a modern camera. But immediately after, the tempo picks up again. The picture-taking becomes the excuse for an impromptu festival; and when I leave, we are all genuinely sorry to say goodbye.

At the southernmost edge of these colorful villages lies Pisa. The Leaning Tower is always the goal of tourists once they reach her train station. But those who board waiting city buses are dropped off at the main entrance to the Campo dei Miracoli and must then run a half-mile gauntlet of souvenir stands, which line the road right up to the *campanile.* These nicknack stalls offer innumerable keychains, ashtrays, and glow-in-the-dark or plug-in-on-top-of-your-television plastic replicas of the famous landmark, in addition to rack after rack of psychedelically tinted, postapocalyptic-looking postcards bearing the image of the Leaning Tower at sunset.

After my first visit, I found that by walking from the station through the quiet, arcaded streets of the lesser-known Pisa, I could avoid the vendors and arrive at the Field of Miracles through the back door. From the top of the tower, the countryside spreads out below: the ancient, crenelated town walls stretching toward the Arno, the river moving slowly through Pisa to the blue line of the Mediterranean in the distance, and the mountains of Carrara to the north bearing long, white gashes from Michelangelo's marble quarries. Directly beneath me, tour book aside, is the true miracle of the Campo: some of the only grass lawn to be found in all of Italy. On this bright green carpet stand the four ivory-colored marble monuments: the renowned *campanile* with its fifteen-foot lean; mammoth cruciform cathedral; frosted wedding-cake baptistery; and the long, low walls of the Campo Santo cemetery—all faced with row upon row of leaping marble arches. The masons who created these mas-

Yellow Wall
Pisa, Italy

terpieces used whatever stones were at hand, including remnants from ruins of the Roman Empire. Now bits of Latin inscriptions, their meanings lost, run at all angles about the walls.

It is a rare day when I have not had to share this breathtaking sight with hundreds of screaming Italian schoolchildren. Often their noise and crowding have pushed me farther and farther toward the vertiginous ledge of polished marble, slippery from recent rainfall. I can easily imagine myself personally proving Galileo's law of gravity as I and other hapless visitors fall at a consistent rate of speed to the bottom of the *campanile,* propelled over the flimsy railings by hordes of kids running free from the supervision of their teachers, who wisely wait below, outside the heavy iron turnstile.

Away from the monuments, crowds quickly diminish. Stone and stucco buildings painted beet red, sulfur yellow, and raw sienna are mirrored in the Arno, the colors enriched by the river fog. Houses lining the peaceful streets are decorated with fountains and carved recesses hiding frescoes or madonnas. Standing alone in empty piazzas are statues of dignitaries commemorating long-forgotten events: eyes ablaze, hands raised with fiery intent, stone robes billowing in an imaginary breeze. The colorful façades are their only audience, pasted thick with layers of black-and-white funeral notices.

Once a great maritime republic, Pisa accumulated vast riches from control of a good part of the Mediterranean's trade until her harbor silted up in the thirteenth century. Most of the wealth was lavished on elaborate building projects such as the Campo dei Miracoli. The city's strong support of architecture continues today. A local ordinance requires that when remodeling uncovers a piece of architectural history, the builder must carefully restore it and leave it exposed. This has transformed many Pisan buildings into beautiful collages of architectural styles in which successive generations are revealed in a single façade, splendid legacies of a city that has been built, rebuilt, ripped apart, and patched up over the centuries.

Down the mountainous inland spine of Italy, clinging to nearly every cliff and ridge, are the fortified hill towns. Some trace Etruscan or Roman origins; but most were founded during the seventh century, when plagues of pirates and malaria drove whole cities from the coastal plains to mountain tops. Isolated, independent, and self-contained, these once impenetrable fortresses drew strength from their formidable sites and the very stone from which they were

Old Stones
Pisa, Italy

Candles
Volterra, Italy

built. Now they stand half-abandoned and languishing, exhausted guardians without a charge.

Unlike the painted villages of the coasts, inland hill towns derive their color mainly from varied local stone. The great perimeter walls and every house, church, tower, and street are constructed exclusively from the rock on which they sit. This lends each town a subtle, overall color and a distinctive character. San Gimignano and Spoleto are warm and inviting golden limestone, while Volterra and Orvieto are dark brown and somber from volcanic tufa. Lighthearted Assisi is jubilant pink marble. Massive gray granite makes Spello and Gubbio impressive though gloomy. Melancholy Sorano and Vitorciano are a distinctive pale gray tufa. And classical Pienza is resplendent in pristine white marble.

Some of the hill towns, like Siena and Perugia, are really hill cities. Here the beauty is found within the walls, in individual monuments and piazzas. But in the far-flung galaxy of small hill villages, beauty is more often discovered from without. Seen from a distance they appear as a Cubist's dream of crisp shapes, half carved, half built, their forms pinned to the cliff face by twin towers of bell and clock.

Both the bus and the poplar-lined road usually stop below the hill on which a town is perched. So, body inclined well forward, I struggle up the rocky path, which ascends by spiraling switchbacks to a narrow gate in the crumbling, grass-grown walls. Inside there is always an imposing but forlorn castle overlooking the stone-paved square, and a church with a few worn details revealing the lost era of prosperity. All around, severe houses precariously crowd the precipice, their rooms piled one atop another, jammed against the fortifications.

To the ever-present echo of tapping, as men chip away at a stone doorframe or loose mortar, I climb through narrow stepped alleys trapped in perpetual shade by high walls. Lethargic dogs eye stray cats that ambivalently stalk caged canaries outside front doors. Children's handmade paper banners announcing an upcoming festival often run across an entry to the piazza, where old people methodically follow the shadow cast by the church tower to escape the burning sun.

There are many reminders that these hill towns, now camouflaged by lack of paint, were much more colorful in the past. Under eaves and arches and in any corner where the sun and rain have lost their power, bits of color cling. Interiors of homes and courtyards are often still gaily colored. But these days, pots of flowers mostly take the place of paint for decoration.

With pirates long vanished and mosquitoes downed by DDT, there is no longer a need to live far from the fertile fields and water of coastal plains. Hill town life is hard, and comforts are minimal. Small-scale farming offers scant reward. The isolation can be overwhelming and is especially cruel in winter, when villagers are

Blue Alcove
Orvieto, Italy

imprisoned in cold stone houses. All year round there is that laborious hill to conquer before reaching fields, market, or home. To discontented youth, hill towns are more jail than refuge; but their understandable exodus drains the villages of vitality. And so, unfortunately, most hill towns seem destined to become ghost towns.

Italy is a very old country. In the southern provinces she can fool no one about her age. All the bones and wrinkles show in this dry and rocky land, weary from long, hard struggle against invaders and the tantrums of nature. Far from established paths of trade and tourism, much of the South is untouched by change and little known, even to other Italians. Locked in a rarefied atmosphere of geographic isolation, religious fervor, and superstition, both spontaneous architecture and vernacular color have thrived.

Catholicism is basic and its rituals primitive throughout the South. There is always a steady stream of pilgrims to any shrine, brought in buses from nearby villages and escorted by their parish priest. Candles gutter in dim chapels before the omnipresent Our Lady of Sorrows, elaborately dressed and bejeweled, weeping profusely as daggers sprout from Her heart. A powerful, agonized Christ rests on purple silk in a glass case, eyes glazed, red paint flowing realistically from all wounds. Here saints are portrayed more gruesomely martyred, their stigmata more numerous, their power to work miracles all the greater.

Votive offerings, hanging from frayed ribbons or tacked to walls, encircle these statues. Tangible prayers of pressed or beaten silver and tin, these *ex-votos* call attention to needs or express thanks for services rendered. The countless metal internal organs, limbs, and livestock, often depicted in odd proportions from warped perspectives, embody vital concerns of health and livelihood. They manifest the intense, unquestioning faith that endures in the South.

Mysticism and superstition are accepted alongside orthodox religious practices without any sense of incongruity. Belief in *malòcchio,* the Evil Eye, persists; and its ominous power remains real and threatening. There is talk of demon possession, werewolves, sorcery, and vampires. Houses where witches live are acknowledged by locals with a hiss and two outstretched fingers to ward off danger, while they spit three times and cross themselves, piling up added precautions. Like the invocation of a saint's favor, spells, charms, and incantations are still more popular and trusted than medical doctors and pharmacies.

Invariably I begin my travels through the South in Naples. Both Sally and I have come to love this city, despite myriad warnings and abundant bad press. True,

Wall of St. Anthony
San Donato, Italy

earplugs are essential; sleep would be impossible amid millions of cars and mopeds sans mufflers roaring up and down the hilly streets throughout the night. But we have never experienced the reported crime nor seen the desperate poverty so often associated with Neapolitans. We have come to know only extremely friendly people and found a dense and vital traditional life with wonderful street markets, hundreds of colorful electrified shrines, and the hottest *penne alla arrabbiata* in Italy.

In the Bay of Naples, near the bubbling, steaming volcanic Campi Flegrei—the fabled entrance to Hell—lies the small island of Procida. Its village of Coricella, a tangle of domes, arcades, and pastel-colored houses, tumbles down a steep hillside to its busy harbor jammed with all colors and sizes of boats. Atop this hill overlooking the bay perches a monastery dedicated to Saint Michael. I had formed a habit of searching out the crypt beneath the altar in Italian churches to view the array of ex-votos and relics that are often assembled in this deepest, oldest layer of the architecture. So even though the monastery's chapel was completely deserted that day, I followed a staircase down into the bowels of the rock from which it was cut, past an ancient library heaped with moldering medieval manuscripts.

The quiet was unsettling. Intermittent slits in the stone wall lent faint light. An open door let me into a storeroom crammed with dusty polychrome saints and angels, gilt processional litters, crumpled paper flowers, and tattered banners. As my eyes adjusted to the shadows, I had the strange feeling that I was not alone; I turned. Grinning up at me from behind a cobwebby iron grill were dozens of skeletons and mummies wrapped in monks' robes. If the bodies of these holy men were being tested for their incorruptibility, then they had most surely failed. Just beyond this gruesome sight was another room with a rich, celestial-blue ceiling painted with cherubs, stars, and a gigantic, knife-studded heart. Below this fantastical sky was an altar lined with skulls whose names were written in beautiful, antiquated script across the craniums. That was enough of the macabre for me. I raced back up the stone steps, through the vacant church, and out into the sunlight.

A general rule holds that the farther south you travel on the Italian peninsula, the slower and less dependable public transportation becomes. In the remote and rugged region of Basilicata, the instep of the boot, trains give up altogether, forsaking one to the frazzled, vibrating buses. I was headed for Matera, capital of the province, to investigate the *sassi,* an elaborate city of cave dwellings.

The rail timetable promised I would reach my bus connection by midday, but the

Hidden Room
Monastery, Procida, Italy

World War I-vintage train, with varnished wooden seats and tiny windows, creaked and rumbled along on a schedule of its own. Unconfirmed rumors of a wildcat strike by railworkers moved faster than the train. After crawling on for hours through the stony, treeless landscape, we stopped in the middle of nowhere. Human crows muffled in sweltering black wool, who seem to tyrannize transport throughout the Mediterranean, decreed that the windows remain jammed shut for fear of *malaria* (bad air). Other passengers, perplexed by the delay, eventually abandoned their airless compartments to picnic in the shade of the rail cars. Some walked off to seek God-knows-what solution in the wilderness. Suddenly the train started up again unannounced. The crowd went wild.

Screaming mothers stuffed baskets and babies through open windows. Men ran alongside, yelling instructions to their wives. Old men, hampered by age, struggled on board, blocking the entry doors with waving canes. Clambering children grabbed the outside handgrips. Then, a few miles down the line, the train shuddered to another mysterious halt, and the earlier drama was replayed.

It was 10:00 P.M. when the train quit at the deserted station of Metaponto, too late to continue my journey. The stationmaster, heading home for the night, took pity on this last, lone tourist of the summer and dropped me off within a mile of an all-but-vacant beach hotel not quite shut for the season. I barely escaped spending eternity here when the bored manager tried to rid my room of mosquitoes by asphyxiating them—and nearly me—with the acrid smoke from a tiny hot plate.

The next day an ancient bus finally consigned me to Matera at sunset. The golden tufa stone of the *sassi* burned magnificent purple as night fell. Kerosene lamps flickered on inside cave houses, and dim streetlights twinkled softly. The pungent smell of grape and olive leavings from recent pressings permeated the town.

Following the oompah-pah of a brass band, I discovered I had arrived just in time for the finale of the grape harvest. A celebration was in full swing. Donkeys pulled farm-carts-turned-festival-floats, draped with crêpe paper and piled high with wine barrels and bunches of grapes. Village girls, decked out in togas with grape-leaf laurels for crowns, presided over the events. Late into the night I marched through the streets with the rest of the population, eating folded pizza and sweet, green grapes.

With the dawn I walked through upper Matera, which is built on a projection over a deep gorge cut by erosion. The town, full of Renaissance buildings and baroque churches, bustles with the business of running the region. A huge cathedral dominates the ridge. Like much of southern Italy, the church is shaken by frequent earthquakes: the dreaded *terremòto* of banner headlines. Without regard for dignity, telephone poles prop up its careening façade. Fallen stone saints are scattered on the ground

Wall with Oratorio
Matera, Italy

all around, lounge chairs for sunning lizards. My usual scrutiny of side streets revealed walls inset with oratorios and washed in amazing colors: violet and apricot, orchid and orange, magenta and chartreuse.

Lining the sheer cliffs below the cathedral is the cave city of *sassi*, often indistinguishable from the rock. Donkeys laden with the harvest clip-clop on narrow paths that zigzag up, over, and around a maze of thousands of houses carved from the soft volcanic stone. For a few hundred lire—about a quarter—a small boy offered to guide me to the tiny, ancient rock churches, monasteries, and convents sprinkled among these homes. Speaking a strange dialect that I eventually realized was his version of English, he pointed out remnants of frescoed icons. These stiff Byzantine figures with uplifted fingers and staring eyes are the only reminders of the sixty thousand Greek monks who fled the eighth-century iconoclasts of their homeland, rather than break their vows. Accustomed to stark accommodations, the exiles carved and frescoed cave towns throughout this region. Only Matera's outlasted the centuries.

Only with overcrowding were the *sassi* living standards lowered, as the caves multiplied and the people continued to dig deeper and deeper into the hillsides. Recently, embarrassed by the primitive conditions, the state built a whole city of nondescript apartment buildings on the nearby plains. Families were relocated, and the caves blocked up to prevent return. But since the latest earthquakes, stable shelters are in short supply and so the solid *sassi* have been reoccupied.

Little explored and least altered, Apulia, on the South's Adriatic Coast, is my favorite region in all of Italy. Running from the spur of the boot down to the tip of the long narrow heel, this land is richly interlaced with oddities in history, custom, and architecture. Apulians are proud of these peculiarities, just as they value personal eccentricities. There is little need here to appear normal, and few seem compelled to adjust to advances of Church, state, or century. This stand-alone spirit, steeped in tradition, unleashes a flood of color.

The coastline of central Apulia is strung with a series of seaports and small fishing towns, little changed since the days of the Crusades. Seven hundred years ago, thousands passed through these Adriatic gates on their way to and from the Holy Land for God's greater glory, or greed. Today, every town from Trani to Otranto retains a massive Norman castle and an intricate Romanesque cathedral cradling the bones of a saint, miraculously oozing oily manna. The church faces are crowded with medieval bestiaries carved from limestone bleached white by the sea. Exotic

Steps and Sea
Trani, Italy

Shrine
Ostuni, Italy

birds, griffins, sea serpents, newts, dwarves, and unicorns coil and writhe around Byzantine bronze doors, bright green from salt spray.

The houses surrounding these monuments are a jumble of decaying stone, the poorest areas splashed with garish color. Down a confusion of cobbled lanes, too stepped and narrow for cars, peddlers heave wheelbarrows piled with fish and produce. Their monotone chants are punctuated by the clap from fishermen beating octopuses tender against the seawall. On stony beaches below, clusters of small, brightly painted boats christened with saints' names for protection, rest in the sun. Some are hung with pairs of huge glass globes, bright acetylene lamps to attract and dazzle fish at night.

Tourist brochures like to pretend that Italy is a continuously warm and sunny country. But by late October, shivering in an unheated, stone-walled *pensione,* I had doubts. Outside my window in the tiny inland hill town of Locorotondo, volunteer firemen were stringing big electric lights in baroque patterns across the one main street in preparation for a religious festival. I could hear the town band practicing, the brittle air amplifying their quick marches and slow military fanfares.

As in much of rural Italy, Apulian public buses are strictly utilitarian, leaving at dawn and returning after dark. They transport laborers to canning factories, farmers to weekly markets, and children to school. Since the weather was cold and uncertain, I decided not to risk a long hike. Up at 5:00 A.M., I found the boarding house door locked and bolted. Rather than wake the innkeeper's family, I climbed out a window and caught the only bus for Ostuni just as it pulled away.

An intricate mound of cubes mounting a hill in a vast plain of wheat, Ostuni is the paragon among the South's dramatic whitewashed villages. That day all was silent within medieval walls. The autumn sun cast long shadows. I could smell the morning bread-baking in progress, but the narrow lanes were empty. Without the burning sun it was built to withstand and with no evidence of her people, Ostuni was an eerie, alien place.

Patches of heavy, black-and-white clouds scudded overhead, but eventually the day warmed, and I set off on a hike. The countryside is especially beautiful here. Rich red, stony soil is dotted with olive and almond trees. Pure red poppies blanket fallow fields. Small parcels of hard-won land are ringed by chest-high walls of loose limestone, forming three-foot-wide lanes winding over the low, undulating landscape. Occasionally a dog barked, calling my attention to a farmer and his donkey working in the groves. By afternoon a hot sun fought the bitterly cold wind. Fortified with pasta, mashed favas, and bitter turnip greens from a remote café, I resumed my walk. I came across a set of life-size, realistically rendered statues of saints gazing heavenward in silence. Across the lane, a magnificently painted gate, crowned by a small broken statue, opened onto a pile of stones.

Sprinkled throughout this rocky land, standing alone or in groups, are the curious, anachronistic *trulli.* These strange, unmortared, dry stone structures with conical roofs once had counterparts throughout the ancient world. But here in Apulia they proliferated and remain, peculiar relics of history and politics.

In the seventeenth century a cruel, ambitious feudal lord known as One-Eyed of Apulia was determined to avoid paying taxes to his nominal master, the king of Spain. Since assessment was based upon the number and value of new buildings in the region, wily One-Eyed outlawed the use of mortar. This forced his subjects to house themselves in rough, loose stone *trulli,* which traditionally had been used only for simple field shelters and storage. At the first sign of a royal accountant, all unreported buildings could quickly be reduced to inconspicuous heaps of rock.

The scheme was effectively administered by threat of torture. Under this oppression *trullisti—trulli*-building specialists—evolved, and finely crafted and detailed dwellings were developed. One day word came of an assessor's imminent appearance. Overnight, whole villages were demolished. The inspector arrived, found nothing, and left, none the wiser. The dwellings were soon reconstructed from the rubble. Eventually the tax evasion was discovered, and One-Eyed was called to Spain, never to return. But in this isolated region the seeds of tradition had taken root. Today, centuries after One-Eyed's law was repealed, his legacy lives on. *Trulli* construction remains the standard building technique in this valley.

Each *trullo* represents several hundred tons of fieldstone, rising in a cone of concentric circles to a carved finial. Five-foot-thick walls with tiny windows and a small, low, arched doorway keep the houses cool but demand that interiors be white-washed to capture and reflect the limited light. This *latte di calcio* (milk of calcium), made from burned limestone, is also used on exterior walls for cleanliness and as painted decoration on roofs. Occasionally, brilliant pigments are added to the white-wash, with striking results.

Trulli cones bear signs and symbols of primitive religious cults. Some date from returning Crusaders. Others have been carried over from prehistoric pagan rites. Crosses, crescents, archaic letters, and spheres, their secret meanings lost, are still copied and repainted year after year.

Brindisi is the gateway to Greece, and most tourists never venture farther south. But beyond this chaotic waiting room of

Painted Gate
Ostuni, Italy

a port town, a road runs along the edge of low stone cliffs toward the *finibus terrae,* the end of the earth. This is the Salentina Peninsula, where the translucent turquoise sea sweeps between limestone headlands and rumbles in caverns hidden below. It amazes me that from the Venetian Lagoon south along five hundred miles of coastline, all buildings, except for the occasional odd extravagance, are left bare, unpainted stone, or whitewashed. Then suddenly, unexpectedly, in this flat, dry, barren land, small villages burst into dazzling color, from luxuriously saturated to delicate pastel.

In the peninsula's center is Lecce, a city of baroque monuments galore, its limestone mansions, churches, and fountains literally dripping with ornament. Here the impressive carving is decoration enough, and painted color is unnecessary. But out in the countryside, lacking impressive building sites or even a church worthy of note, the villagers respond. They bring out the paint buckets, hiding their humble buildings and poverty under coats of affordable brilliance.

When I asked people in the Salentine villages why they paint their homes bright colors, I was told again and again that it has always been done this way and that is the way they like it. In San Donato all the doors are chocolate brown, in Squinzano and Trepuzzi, only patina green. And so it goes, always the same reason: tradition, its origins forgotten.

An old woman invited me into her little café in San Donato. The old stone, double-barrel vault was painted cerise and aqua with canary yellow trim. A bare light bulb, a couple of oilcloth-covered tables, mismatched but brightly painted wooden chairs, and a calendar sporting a long-suffering saint were the only decorations. She sat me down and poured a glass of *aranciata* as an excuse to ask where I was from and why I was there. All day the object of curiosity and suspicion, I had noticed faces obscured by dark interiors, peering from behind blinds and peeking out of shuttered windows, observing me while I worked. She probably satisfied the entire village with my answers.

Joining me in a snack of prickly pears, peeling back the studded green skin to reach the sweet, pink fruit, she lamented that while San Donato had been there forever, there was nothing noteworthy to show for the past: no great cathedral, no ancient monument. But had I been to Lecce? *"Che bella, bella, bellissima!"* she sang. But here in San Donato, it was poor, there was nothing. Just a small village—abounding in glorious color.

France

For centuries the French have dictated manners and fashions, led the world in philosophy, and fostered political ideals. Pioneers of science and industry, they also stimulated major movements in art, design, and architecture. But urbane style, elegant ideas, and technological advances do not nurture tradition. Now, in this civilized land of Concordes and *haute cuisine,* most provincial life and color have gone the way of the ox-drawn plow.

Historically the bridge between northern and southern Europe, France presided over the meeting of Germanic and Latin cultures as the northernmost outpost of the Mediterranean soul. Today the country looks almost wholly to the North, with Paris setting the pace and style. Little remains of Latin influence but the root of the language, a few scattered Roman ruins, and a tiny strip of the Riviera, which still looks toward the Mediterranean Sea rather than the capital for inspiration.

It is difficult to imagine how important a role painted color once played in the architecture of France. But clues can be found in the flecks of brilliant pigment that still cling to the nooks and carvings of her monuments. Churches, monasteries, and even the great Gothic cathedrals were once lavishly decorated inside and out, their walls and statuary painted, gilded, and patterned in ruby red, cobalt blue, and royal purple, colors equally vivid as their parallels in stained glass.

Ultimately, paint that was not washed away by the elements was meticulously scraped from walls and ornament during church reform movements seeking simplicity

Boulangerie
Villefranche, France

Rue du Palmier
Menton, France

and austerity. What little color then remained was destroyed during the French Revolution by looters who mistook painted statues wearing crowns of everlasting life for representations of detested earthly royalty. Simple French houses, as depicted by early artists, were also more colorful. But this tradition was lost over time without churches to reinforce the beauty and use of color.

The streets of France today are not altogether lackluster. Paint enriches shopfronts and signage throughout the nation. But these elaborate, professional displays are not the innocent, spontaneous expressions I seek. They are a refined, studied art. A few isolated pockets of provincial color do remain. In Colmar on the German border, ancient, leaning half-timbered houses are painted in soft shades, but in a style more Swiss-German than Mediterranean. And in the village of Roussillon in Provence, a stroll through town coats my shoes in a rainbow of colored dust. Here ocher is mined for paint manufacture, and the earth yields intense pigments of orange, yellow, lavender, and red. Houses are built of the local variegated stone or covered with stucco made from the richly tinted soil. But these towns are rare niches of color. Their neighbors revert to the raw limestone and gray stucco so characteristic of France.

The whitewash of Spain spills into France from the west, just as color bleeds across the French border from Italy into the Côte d'Azur. Along this slim stretch of coastline, a perpetual stream of narcissistic sun worshipers floods the cosmopolitan beaches and casinos of the international resorts. While I can appreciate the beauty of the water and the strength of the sun, the impressionists' light is not a part of my work. So I spend my time walking during the day and photographing at dusk in the older, less pretentious quarters behind the Riviera's glitter, where both vernacular color and a quieter, if abridged, traditional life continue.

Just to the east of Nice's palm-fringed avenues of palatial hotels and luxury boutiques is her old town, crowded untidily onto a hilly promontory. Here, lavishly dressed and undressed tourists mingle with workmen in blue coveralls carrying fresh baguettes and flowers. Fishermen deliver their catch, produce sellers stack ripe plums and peaches in pyramids under boldly striped canvas awnings, and brightly robed and turbaned North Africans peddle ivory trinkets. All are set magnificently against stuccoed walls of salmon, apricot, and celery green. One little French boy, watching me photograph, boasted that all the colors of Nice had been specially selected by his grandfather who had painted each and every house.

Down the coast the tiny, color-washed houses of Villefranche tumble to a deep turquoise harbor pinched between malachite mountains. And within sight of Italy, just behind the flash of its beachfront, Menton's polychrome baroque churches and homes in fragile tints belie French rule.

Broken Cross
Carcassonne, France

Statue and Sign
Carcassonne, France

Pink Wall with Clothespins
Villefranche, France

Spain

White dominates Spain. The intensely burning sun with its blinding white glare seems to bleach the color from everything. It blanches the Spanish earth, rendering an albino landscape of dust and stone littered with desiccated villages of brilliantly whitewashed boxes.

It was not always so. Surprisingly, both the colorless land and architecture stem from centuries-old political decisions. Spain was once fertile green, but for hundreds of years kings granted the powerful guild of sheep owners free rein. In their seasonal wanderings, vast flocks trampled crops and stripped all vegetation from the central plateau. Eventually the denuded land could no longer hold moisture, and the very climate of Spain was changed forever. Wind stole the topsoil, devastating agriculture; to this day the impoverished farming peasantry have not recovered. Now a parched, treeless wasteland sweeps between a thin band of orchards following the Mediterranean coast and the green, pine-covered Pyrenees.

Spanish architecture was once also much more colorful. But the brilliant paint and tile from more than a thousand years of Roman and Moorish occupations have largely been abandoned. An architect in Ronda gave me a plausible, if perhaps apocryphal, explanation for this lack of color in Spain's buildings today. He told of the enlightened eighteenth-century reformist monarch, Carlos III, who was horrified by the rampant epidemic diseases scourging his subjects. He handed down a royal edict, requiring that all houses in his domain be limewashed every spring. This

Hostal
Seville, Spain

Moorish Door
Seville, Spain

white coat provided an effective, inexpensive, readily available disinfectant; and health was promoted, even though neither the workings of the milky paint nor infection were understood. Dirty whitewash could not be disguised, and so annual compliance was easily monitored. The law took hold, severing the legacy of color, and Spain's *pueblos blancos* were born.

In the far north near Barcelona, color is exerted in the surrealist tilework of the architect Antonio Gaudí, and in the utopian communities designed by his successors, the vivid colorists of the Bofill atelier. But in most of Spain, whitewash and bare stone are relieved only by a profusion of flowers. Mandarin and crimson bougainvillea climb hot, chalky walls, purplish fuchsias weep in corners near splashing fountains that cool the air, and pots of pink geraniums hang on iron hoops from blind façades. Occasionally, colorful glazed tiles perpetuating Arabic designs wink from secluded courtyards. Painted color, however, is marooned in the town's gypsy quarter or ostracized altogether.

Because of the sparsity of color, I am not enticed to spend much time in Spain or France. My impressions of both are therefore limited; and like all travelers, I am prone to jump to false conclusions from brief visits, only to alter them with experience. As yet, I find I am not enchanted by the Spaniards. Here most everyone, rich or poor, has the dignity and pretension of an aristocrat. Ritualized manners refined through generations, however, do not apply to many aspects of modern life. Spaniards will not stand in line. A reservation is worthless on a bus or train, where early claim is essential to avoid finding someone planted firmly and finally in my seat. Never mind the NO FUMADO marker in the smoke-filled compartment or the unacknowledged stop sign on the road. In post-Franco Spain, practical rules for community comfort, safety, and health are simply ignored in a spree of long-repressed freedom. And so the pride and arrogance of conquistadors combine with today's reigning spirit of *viva yo* (hooray for me) to express more interest in show than substance, and self than society.

Traditional Spanish villages appear much like the people: majestic, dignified, indifferent, and vain. From a distance these towns are great fortified medieval cities. But behind battered, overgrown walls in what were once thriving communities stand only scattered, tumbledown houses with sagging, rippling clay tile roofs stepping up to broken castles. The tangled streets are overseen by resident storks, beaks clattering. A sign of good fortune throughout the Mediterranean, the bulky birds reign awkwardly from untidy nests atop crumbling towers. Dusty mules bray among patches of rocky stubble where some farmer has managed to grow a little wheat or corn in a burnt pocket of soil. Wood smoke and the smell of frying *churros* fill the air. Dry, brown

Wall with Palm
Seville, Spain

palm leaves, blessed by the Pope at Eastertime, are braided into balcony railings as protection from lightning. Prosperity lives on only in church interiors or in salvaged ornament embedded in whitewashed walls.

Only in early evening do these villages come to life. Their oversized plazas, ringed with acacia trees and whitewashed benches, host the ritual nightly *paseo,* a holdover from the seventeenth century when the aristocracy took the evening air. Girls meet, kiss, and admire one another's shoes and dresses, then promenade, circling in giggling cliques. Teenage boys eye the girls while slouched by the carved stone fountain. Sometimes they join the parade, but tradition keeps them segregated from their destined future brides. Always one boy comes roaring up on a new motor scooter, revving the engine to attract envious eyes and all ears. *Tapas* bars display their snacks to window shoppers awaiting dinner, which, like everything else in Spain, is late.

Along Spain's Mediterranean coast, the past and traditions are less a cherished inheritance than a burden, uncomfortably borne. Here, in an impetuous rush toward the twentieth century, industrialization and furious development have been eagerly embraced. Expanding too fast and too freely, Spain has seen most of her beautiful seaside villages disappear, buried under tourist hotels and discos. Now the whole coastline is a dreary, solid seawall of buildings from Barcelona to Gibraltar. Former fishermen and their families are locked inland, living in vast apartment blocks with no view of the sea, waiting tables or selling suntan lotion and beach balls.

Gypsies bring color with them to Spain. In their claptrap quarters, color explodes: raw, shocking, and primitive. This is transplanted color, out of place and character in the austere Spanish culture. I had read about an especially thriving gypsy settlement in the Andalusian port town of Almería, so I grabbed a southbound train.

When traveling I have found that it is often possible to judge the sincerity of a new friend or a stranger's advice by the vigor of their warnings. Now, as I passed through the countryside, I was continually and vehemently admonished to beware of gypsies. Approaching Almería, predictions of my fate became more gruesome. *"¡Banditos, banditos!"* the elderly Spanish couple sharing my compartment cautioned. They whispered wide-eyed of stolen babies, wallets, and gold and mimed slashed throats and missing fingers. Instructing me to follow their sage example, they vigilantly removed wedding rings and jewelry and sat on all their valuables. Waving a heavy cane, the husband gestured that he was prepared.

Upon our arrival I could see clusters of brightly painted houses stuck like barnacles to the cliffs above town. This is the seedy gypsy district known as the Chanca. Entering against all counsel, I never felt wholly comfortable here; but I suspect this was due more to the horror stories than any real menace.

Portrait Shop
Madrid, Spain

With one eye always on the lookout, it was impossible for me to miss the short, fleshy gypsy woman of indeterminate age and tonnage flaring behind me in tight purple slacks and a loose, chrome-yellow flowered blouse. She watched me work for half an hour, hands on her hips, asking questions in a loud, gravelly voice. I sensed she saw some opportunity in me, but I could not determine precisely what that was. Herself a blazing palette, she shared my interest in color and dragged me to see her one-room, lime-green stone hut. Over her doorway she had painted the words *Hay Mañana* in vibrating turquoise. Whether interpreted as procrastination or hope, this was obviously her life's theme.

Inside, a mangy lapdog pranced wildly about. Her orange bedspread was strewn with dozens of frayed souvenir pillows and carnival dolls, the groaning vanity cluttered with bottles of colored water, costume jewelry, and dusty bunches of gaudy, fadeless plastic flowers. Glossy magazine clippings of singers and soap-opera idols were taped to her peeling mirror. Without provocation she began to dance, writhing emotionally to the whining music blaring from a nearby café, clapping her hands and stomping her feet in a bizarre variation on flamenco. I escaped when a shady character in mirrored sunglasses and polyester pants entered and spontaneously joined in her mysterious rite. *Hay mañana* indeed.

Far removed in spirit from the Chanca, my favorite spot in all of Spain is not very colorful, Mediterranean, or Spanish. It is the Cantabrian coast of northern Spain, a damp blend of sea and mountain, where streams cut rolling green fields dotted with fattening cows. In this lush landscape, which receives the rain denied the rest of Spain, sleeps the village of Santillana del Mar. It rose up around a monastery sheltering the relics of Saint Juliana, a fourth-century virgin martyr from whom the town derives its name. During the Middle Ages, Santillana was a goal for thousands of pilgrims who paused here on their way to the shrine of Santiago de Compostela. Later the village became a favorite retreat of Spanish aristocracy seeking relief from summer heat. Eventually abandoned by privileged and pious alike, Santillana today is a small dairy farming community, little changed in the last three hundred years.

It was late April and raining hard. All night long a freezing wind rattled the wooden shutters of the small room I had rented from a Santillana farmer. Since it was officially no longer winter, his house of rough stucco-covered stone went unheated. The floor, built of huge, heavy timber, was darkly aged and worn from centuries of footsteps. The only furnishings were a massive carved bed, a simple stool, and an elegant gilded crucifix hanging on the whitewashed wall.

In early morning, ringing bells and the smell of wet wood smoke found their way through the paneled shutters and past the double set of windows used to combat

Gypsy House
Chanca, Almería, Spain

Wall with Crest
Santillana del Mar, Spain

Shop Wall
Santiago de Compostela, Spain

the cold. I reluctantly emerged from the protection of a thick wool blanket and hurried down the scalloped stone steps to a nearby café for a breakfast of crusty bread, fresh-churned butter, and the potent hot chocolate of Spain. There I listened to the local farmers complain about the weather. Slowly the cold rain turned to a gentle mist, and I set off toward the nearby Altamira caverns.

I threaded my way past milk cows being herded to pasture through the center of town. A man, hunched into a heavy black coat and Basque beret, prodded them down the cobbled street lined with stone and stucco mansions of the long-departed blue bloods of Castile. Over the heads of his oblivious beasts loomed ancient family coats of arms. Life-size Renaissance nobles and knights in armor leapt from the stone shields, displaying more bravado than old walls should ever be forced to bear.

A woman wrapped in a lace shawl and patterned apron sold me a glass of fresh milk, just as her ancestors must have done for a thousand years of pilgrims. Beneath a stone crest over the moss-grown archway, her withered mother and plaid-skirted daughter sat at a wooden table pouring warm milk from beaten metal pitchers. Each evening at milking time I would see the trio meeting their herd: black-and-white, palace-bound cows returning slowly, bells clanking.

I passed a husband and wife cutting hay in a jade-green field dressed with blue wildflowers. He wielded a great scythe while she gathered and tied the harvest into bundles. The air was impregnated with the scent of new-cut grass and thyme. Cave openings could be seen everywhere. I followed a lane to some of the oldest and most beautiful color in the world, the prehistoric paintings of bison stampeding through the Altamira caves. There on the walls were the ancient colors, applied by the light of burning animal fat: white from chalky stone, black from charcoal, red from rusty iron ore, natural ocher, and blue from copper-laced stone, all still as vibrant as they were fifteen thousand years ago.

Cloud Wall
Santillana del Mar, Spain

Portugal

Locked in a tiny, remote corner of the vast Iberian Peninsula between hostile Spain and the Atlantic, Portugal has always looked to the sea. There, in quick succession, the Portuguese discovered, possessed, and then lost much of the world and its riches. Today, humbled by their squandered chance, they are simple fishermen and farmers, the keepers of tradition watching over remnants of past glory.

European travelers inevitably fall into two distinct camps. There are those seduced by Spain's pomp and grandeur; and others, like me, devoted to Portugal. The two countries make such an extraordinary contrast that it is difficult to believe only a border separates them. Cross into Portugal at any point along the frontier, and the pace of life abruptly slows down. Villages are suddenly cleaner and quieter. Most are settled peacefully in valleys rather than perched militantly atop hills, as are the towns of her predominant neighbor. Portugal's landscape is also less dramatic. Compared to Spain's brutal desolation, Portugal is pastoral and tame. But what entices me is the color, which unexpectedly flourishes here. Great houses are washed in delicate pinks. Rural cottages bloom in tantalizing hues or are cloaked in boldly patterned and colored tiles. Even the boats along her rivers, flooded rice fields, and seacoast are always gaily painted, often with great, unblinking eyes on the prow to search the depths for fish while simultaneously staring down the Evil Eye.

Fisherman's House
Costa Nova, Portugal

Azulejos
Faro, Portugal

The Portuguese spirit is gentle and unpretentious. Community retains its meaning and importance. Though the people are certainly poor, they are instinctively hospitable and generous; and the virtues of hard work, patience, moderation, and simple good manners are honored and respected. Food, clothing, and shelter are all basic and ordinary. The Portuguese are not enamored of novelty nor are they eager to change. The modern world is not much in evidence. Few public clocks can be found, for time means little, even in Lisbon. The great simplicity of life here is not due to poverty alone, but to a state of mind under the spell of another age.

In Portugal history is palpable. Nearly three thousand years ago seafaring Phoenicians settled the coast; their influence can still be seen in the long, curved prows of boats. Later, Celtic invaders left their mark in the bagpipe music of shepherds, the curious plaids of Nazaré, and the intricate, interwoven patterns and crosses found in tessellated marble pavements. Romans built roads and bridges, many still in use today, while five centuries of Moorish occupation contributed elaborate irrigation systems, a love of gardening, chimney pots pierced with arabesque designs, and tilework.

Especially tilework.

Today, whole streets and villages are dressed in brightly colored glazed ceramic tiles. Palaces, public buildings, train stations, factories, fountains, and even the walls of churches are ornamented. These are Portugal's *azulejos*, from the Arabic *azulejo* (smooth). The earliest were deeply embossed with geometric patterns. Later, whole scenes and narratives were assembled from hand-painted and -fired tiles. Now made generally affordable by machine production, *azulejos* have become the most prevalent means of decorating buildings—more common than paint. They cover even the most humble fisherman's house, and those cottages that are simply painted have at least a small inset of tiles portraying a saint above the door.

After the Moors were eventually ousted and prolonged wars with Spain won, fifteenth-century Portugal became an independent kingdom. Her Mediterranean shipping and trading wrecked by North African pirates, Portugal led the rest of Europe in seeking alternative routes to India and Eastern wealth. Great voyages, culminating in Magellan's round-the-world junket, brought her colonies, and colonies generated vast riches. Portugal soon controlled more than one-third of the known world, and Lisbon became the wealthiest city in Europe, surpassing even Venice.

Portugal's unique Manueline architecture, named after the country's then-reigning king, was born during this age of caravels and exploration. Fascination with the sea and far-off lands was reflected in the ropes, seaweed, anchors and oars, nets and knots, coral, marine beasts, astronomical instruments, tobacco leaves, corncobs, and Indians that twist, twine, and foliate up columns and around windows

Running Girl
Lagos, Portugal

and doorways in this strange, exotic stonework. When gold and diamonds poured in from Brazil, the building boom proliferated with the even more elaborate style of baroque. This period, which owes its name to the Portuguese word *barroco* (rough pearl), ushered in buildings full of grandiose curves and movement.

Like a stunned lottery winner completely unprepared for riches and fame, Portugal gained too much wealth too quickly. She soon set sail on an abortive crusade to capture Morocco. In the course of one afternoon, most of Portugal's nobility were killed, the few survivors ransomed for the contents of the bulging treasury. The country was left leaderless. Without direction, the Portuguese misused, wasted, and for the most part frittered away their prosperity in a flurry of decadence. Everything was too easy. They could buy whatever they wanted, so why work? Agriculture, industry, and crafts toppled into ruin through neglect, never again to regain vitality, while the people reveled in idleness.

The great earthquake of 1755 broke the magic season. It struck on All Saint's Day, when churches were crowded for morning mass. Fire spread from toppled candles and engulfed the capital. In six minutes half of Lisbon was destroyed and most of Portugal devastated. Survivors who rushed to safety in the Targus River were drowned in a tidal wave. Nothing until the 1917–18 appearances of the Virgin Mary—which transformed the sleepy village of Fátima into a swollen center of mass pilgrimage—has so greatly affected the country. To this day Portugal has yet to recover from either event.

Stretching across southern Portugal is the Algarve, ancient paradise of Moorish poets. The vegetation is Mediterranean, the heat African, the light strong and luminous. Along the coast natural bridges of purple rock wade from yellow sand into the technicolor blue-green ocean. Prickly cacti and agaves, carob trees, and palms should dominate this dry, barren soil, but in places where the earth has been brought to life by water from timeless wells, the Algarve is transformed into a luxuriant garden. Roses and oleander bloom beside vineyards. Scarlet poppies run riot over fallow fields and sprout beneath every almond and orange tree. Along the narrow lanes, long-horned oxen pull brightly decorated farm carts and villagers gather snails for afternoon snacks.

A road rolls across the Algarve from the Spanish border past tiny fishing and farming communities toward the Sagres Peninsula. There it narrows to a crawl and continues on through a few scattered, gaudily painted hamlets huddling close to the earth in the incessant wind. It finally dies at the *fim de mundo*, the archaic end of the world, where the sea swallows up the sun each evening. The religions of Portugal's

past are recalled in the place names nearby. The Valley of the Jews nestles among Purgatório, Santa Catarina, and Tunis, all burning in the Algarve sun.

Sadly, much of the Algarve coastline is falling under attack from furious development. Tiny painted fishing communities, which delighted me with their colors and traditions ten years ago, are now being encircled and suffocated by high-rise holiday apartments. Large, ostentatious villas elbow their way between the small, simple, native farmhouses. These are the monstrous progeny of the same speculators who have already ravaged the coast of Spain with a solid wall of condominiums.

Farms, even whole villages are bought up. What is not demolished is whitewashed over to match preconceptions of a Mediterranean resort. This attempt to superimpose an ersatz Spain onto Portugal proceeds with total disregard for the beauty of the indigenous buildings. Developers transplant the complex white villas of the Costa del Sol—curved walls, peaked tile roofs, and all—snubbing the plain, low, squarish, flat-roofed cottages ornamented with *azulejos* and brightly painted plasterwork. Fortunately, just a few miles inland from the coveted coast, authentic Portuguese life and buildings endure.

Away from the beaches, old ways hold fast; and Catholicism, with its incarnate symbol, the church, is at the heart of all traditions, tying together family, village, and country. Here the people's daily exposure to Renaissance and baroque churches, great decorative storehouses for the traditional use of color, has bred a beautiful vernacular architectural expression when translated directly to their houses.

Over a hundred years ago near the hill town of Loulé, homes were often painted with *fingidos* (false work), an imitation marbling of the front façade borrowed in technique and coloring from church interiors. Some of these decorated houses remain intact, scattered about the arid landscape in the isolated rural villages of this district. The *fingidos* give these tiny, humble farmhouses a formality and grandeur far beyond their scale and function.

The individual styles of the *fingidos* painters are readily discernible. Some are crude and almost comic, with trembling, vermiculated scribbles. Others are much more realistic and precise in their veining. Still others are multicolored and abstract, splendidly reminiscent of Florentine marbled papers. Each painter worked within a small territory, often covering a row of houses with slight variations on their characteristic palette and technique. *Fingidos* artists gained their skills from church building and renovation tasks, undoubtedly their primary occupation. The Portuguese have another word for false marble, *escaiola*, which also denotes plaster and stucco. *Escaiola* has its root in the Italian word *scagliuola*, which gives credence to a story I was told that this craft was imported with Italian artisans. Similar to the art of fresco painting on fresh plaster, this false marbling required extensive training and many materials. It was therefore a difficult and costly process, and so usually only the fronts of houses were commissioned while the sides were painted or simply whitewashed.

About fifty years ago, because of some combination of expense, a decline in its popularity, and a break in the tradition of handing down this master craft, the distinctive house painting ceased. As years of hot Algarve sun fade the colors and crack the plaster, many of the buildings that remain continue to deteriorate, so that evidence of this wonderful vernacular art form will soon be lost. Few artisans today are knowledgeable enough in the techniques to manage repairs; and it is very difficult to find anyone, young or old, even among architects and building professionals, who acknowledges these special houses, knows their history, or laments their passing. Even though *fingidos* are poorly documented and disappearing, those remaining are proud possessions of present owners. Their decorated cottage is one of the few opulent and extravagant expressions within a daily environment defined by utility and necessity.

Sometimes the farmers are embarrassed by the ruinous condition of their crumbling façade. One woman dismissed hers with a wave of the hand saying, "Not that, it's old, *está velho*." But all are clearly delighted by my interest. They are honored to have their house photographed, for they feel its beauty brings them respect and recognition. With awe they stress how difficult it would be to duplicate the walls. "It's not easy, *não é fácil*." I told an old farmer that we have nothing like *fingidos* on our houses in the United States. "Oh," he puzzled, and then with sincere pity inquired, "You have no artists in America?"

Every major city has an old quarter that clings to the past. In Lisbon it is the ancient Alfama, housing a dense population in a hilly, tight-knit neighborhood of twisting alleyways, steep steps, and entrenched habits. Saved from the great earthquake by its rock foundation, the Alfama would look familiar to a twelfth-century Crusader but for the sea of television antennas, which rise above the pink, white, yellow, and green painted and tiled façades climbing the cliff over the Targus.

A motley throng jostles within. Hawkers push "lucky" lottery numbers, barking their sevens and twelves; sailors trade risqué tunes; and weathered fishermen emerge from smokey *bodegas*. The air is thick with the smell of charcoal fires, fried fish, and aging wine. Armies of children run screaming through the shadow-thin lanes, dodging blind pencil sellers and gum vendors. Bands of stray dogs beg for scraps

Old Tile
Alfama, Lisbon, Portugal

from café owners. In the marketplace displays of fruits from orchard, garden, and sea vie for attention. Women gather to wash clothes in the public fountain. Older girls embroider while the young ones cut paper carnations for saints' days. Chickens scratch about, one leg tied with string to a chair, while disoriented city roosters crow over the noise, ignorant of the hour for which they are responsible.

On the outskirts of Lisbon, in the no-man's-land of the railroad right-of-way, are clusters of gaily painted makeshift houses following the track for miles. Nearby loom faceless, colorless apartment blocks built to replace these slapdash towns. Together they swallow up the original tiny villages that lend them their names, and stand as daily reminders of the hundreds of thousands of Portuguese refugees who poured into the country after the bloodless coup of the 1970s granted independence to her last colonies.

Drawn to the feast of colloquial color in these exploding suburbs, I was especially captivated by Cruz de Pedra. Here life was in transition. As the squatters were pushed into sanitized, government-sponsored high rises, the simple cottages they had built, tiled, and painted, now deemed substandard eyesores, were steadily being demolished. Revealed when walls toppled and interiors were ripped open was a collage of radiant fields of color. Jewel boxes of ruby red, turquoise, lapis and sapphire blues, emerald, topaz, amethyst, and jade enriched the poor in ways the new bureaucratic projects never could.

People who had always lived close to the earth were now ten stories in the sky. They must have longed for the land, privacy, color, and a place that was truly their own. While I worked, Sally watched them make frequent trips to the ruins of their former homes to pick flowers blooming among the shambles. Some still managed carefully tended gardens next to their vanished cottages. Families continued to take their evening stroll down familiar lanes, sustaining friendships, community, and customs not possible in dark, narrow hallways. Boys played soccer in the former market square or scavenged among the debris as teenagers talked and courted behind collapsing walls their parents had once emblazoned with color.

East of Lisbon, stone-built towns bake in a rain-starved land of glacial winters and blindingly fierce summers. Only cork oaks and sparse crops struggle against the rocky soil. The gem of this region is Estremoz. There is an innocent, antique quality to this village of small, crisply whitewashed houses. These have few if any windows, to fight the sun, while large, projecting chimneys presage the cold months. Wide wooden doors are carefully painted in all tints of the spectrum. Occasionally, bright bands of color disguise wear along the base of walls. Further ornamenting the white façades are brilliantly glazed flowerpots, dangling strings of carmine red peppers, and fantastical birdcages crafted by the village barber. Crickets, little

Abandoned House
Cruz de Pedra, Portugal

Wall with Roses
Obidos, Portugal

Green Door
Estremoz, Portugal

good-luck charms, trill in their own small painted cages, inspiring canaries to sing.

Early each morning Estremoz women furiously scrub the snow-white dust from their front steps and the mosaic stone pavement of their hilly streets. They beat rag rugs to death, stopping only to wave at neighbors or gossip. Little girls, many named Isabel after the pious and generous Queen Saint who died here, play a complicated skipping game, dancing between bands of elastic.

Just up the street from the Queen's chapel, a little old woman, withered and bent by her ninety years, pulled me into her home. She was proud of her house, kept like a museum. All around were the precious mementos and relics of her life mounted on soft blue walls. Odd dolls and dishes adorned the open cupboards. There was a postcard of the Pope, a plaque from Fátima, a water jar from Lourdes, a *relicário* painstakingly decorated by nuns, and hand-tinted photographs of her relatives, the children she had outlived, and the son who never came to visit. In the most prominent position was a strange and incongruous pair. A flowery painting of the Queen Saint wreathed in dried roses was inexplicably allied with a large glossy autographed publicity photo of Lucille Ball, circa 1950. An exotic celluloid "Santa Lucia," smiling her cocky smile from a simple wooden frame.

Northern Portugal is a much greener place. The interior holds the source of many rivers in mist-covered mountains of pine. Granite villages hide among tremendous boulders or repose placidly, encircled by pastures where horses and cattle browse. Along the northern coast are a wide scattering of quiet fishing villages, most untouched by tourism.

One of these, the watery, canal-laced city of Aveiro, sits at the edge of a marshy lagoon, an eerie domain of low, mist-shrouded isles and swampy inlets reaching inward for miles like long, curved fingers. With enormous wooden rakes, locals harvest iodine-rich seaweed—a valuable fertilizer—loading it into narrow boats with pointed, swan-necked prows and sterns painted in bright, primitive designs. Viewed through the gray-green fog, the boats seem to glide on meadows of tall grass and reeds, drifting and grazing like gigantic prehistoric seabirds.

Stranded on a narrow strip of sand between the Atlantic and the lagoon, Costa Nova do Prado makes its living gathering salt, black crabs, and huge eels. The village is formed of vibrantly painted stuccoed huts with curious good-luck symbols, bizarre statuary, and crudely rendered saints over the wide doors. In summer, when the sun burns away the mist from Costa Nova, vacationing Portuguese families fill a collection of small wooden cabins uniquely striped with vertical bands of harlequin colors. Looking like canvas beach cabanas on the sand, these holiday retreats must be painted frequently and liberally against the constant damp Atlantic wind. In the process stiff gusts splash and splatter color upon color.

Ruins
Murtosa, Portugal

Further north, Póvoa de Varzim holds a large old fishing community up against a small modern town. The fishermen live in rows of tiny single-story houses, tiled and painted in an infinite variety of colors and designs. Like traditional villagers throughout the Mediterranean basin, whether farmers toiling long hours in stony fields or fishermen fighting the harsh, unpredictable sea, the Póvoans have had their fill of nature by day's end and do not wish to invite her home. As if to shout defiance, they cover their houses in bold, unnatural colors and patterns. Glossy walls of mass-produced tiles in hot pink, primary yellow, iridescent purple, and lurid rouge, freckled with "new wave" slashes, squiggles, checks, flecks, and polka dots, stop nature at the threshold.

For several weeks I used this town as my base from which to visit nearby villages. Each evening as I walked along the shore, fishermen were just taking to sea in heavy wooden boats, breaking through rough surf to lay nets for the night's catch. Cheers and chanting announced their dawn return. Wives and grandmothers, robust, thick-ankled, and barefoot, met their men on the beach. With a pail of squirming fish in each hand and a big basketful balanced atop their heads, the women carried the harvest to market in the early light, contributing to the writhing mass of sea life sold or traded in a noisy, congested, incomprehensible ceremony. Glistening fish were held up with pride and passed from hand to hand as the auctioneer shouted prices and weights in rapid staccato. The rest of the day nets were mended, boats caulked and retouched, and small fry salted and hung on lines to dry in the breeze like tiny articles of lamé clothing.

The Atlantic is violent and unforgiving. It is not uncommon for boats to be lost and men drowned within sight of the women who watch and wait motionless on the shore. Several times I have been startled by terrifying screams and frightful howls that split the air. I would look to the beach where a grieving widow shouted curses heavenward before withdrawing to wrap herself in eternal black. Most winters it is simply too dangerous to go to sea, so for several months boats sit idle, filling the streets in the fishing quarter. Suddenly mourning cloth multiplies as seasonal "widows" don black to await their husbands' return from less risky work out of town.

The Portuguese year is strung on a series of festivals. An endless line of fairs, processions, pilgrimages, and celebrations glorify saint and season. One year when Sally and I reached Póvoa de Varzim, we found it preening for the final holiday in June, which honors Saint Peter the Fisherman. Garlands of lights, nautical banners, tinfoil boats, and colorful ribbons festooned the streets. Improvised, ramshackle stages trimmed with nets, oars, and rigging created naive backdrops for life-size papier-mâché Peters dressed in rough fishing garb.

Sky Wall
Espinho, Portugal

Bilheteira
Póvoa de Varzim, Portugal

Icon Wall
Póvoa de Varzim, Portugal

Walking at sunset, we heard a slow drum beat accompanied by low cries. Around the corner appeared a great procession. Boys with tall candles heralded a luxuriantly robed priest swinging a smoking censer. Church relics and crowns of silver, presented on black velvet cushions, were reverently escorted by somber acolytes. In the moist, heavy air, ornate tapestries hung limply from tasseled brass posts. Behind, ringed by children with dripping tapers, marched a group of church elders shouldering an empty black carved coffin, draped with flowers and lace. Trailing were hundreds of large, realistically molded heads held high and bobbing on tall wooden poles. These frugal votives made of simple wax recalled the dead beloved of the moaning, sobbing townsfolk dressed in black. Onlookers strewed the path of the procession with rushes and herbs. As the crowd advanced, the scent of crushed mint and thyme mingled with saccharine incense.

Soon wild street festivities, more pagan than Christian, broke the solemn mood. Green wine flowed, and the Disciple was soon forgotten as villagers carrying torches ran singing and screaming through dark, narrow alleys. Near the decorated platforms, people danced around huge bonfires. The bravest jumped through the flames to loud cheering. We feasted on heaps of fresh grilled sardines while skyrockets shattered the night into a million bits of colored light.

Wax Votives
Vila do Conde, Portugal

Morocco

Within sight of Spain but a world away, Morocco is an exotic, polygamous marriage of Europe, Africa, and Arabia, a unique fusion of the Mediterranean, Atlantic, and Sahara. Nodding both East and West, it is a nation of Islam and French pastries, of Berber tribesmen and Arab elite, of kasbahs, camels, ogee arches, and Renaults, sultans, cassette players, and date palms. But to me, Morocco is color—wild, exuberant, tropical, intense. It is a land the color of fruit and flowers, with rose clay and saffron sand, where houses are washed in sultry shades of hibiscus blooms and ripe watermelon or stained the tints of poppies and bleeding pomegranates.

Veiled village women emerge from these richly painted and patterned dwellings to sail up rust red roads before a visible pink wind. Swaddled in layers of florid cloth, they are a whirl of flame, lemon, and peacock blue shot with violet and gold threads. Fluorescent yellow stockings in a pair of fuchsia slippers peek from beneath the wrappings. Out of this shimmering mirage come glimpses of the unguarded left eye, the occasional flash from a gold-toothed smile framed by indigo tattoos, or a coffee-colored hand embroidered with henna. Looking like ruffled parrots on their way to some phantasmagoric prom, they are in fact off to fields or market. Meanwhile, immobile Moroccan menfolk, draped in striated robes and turbans of apricot, lilac, or pale pear green, squat motionless in any available shadow, composing prismatic appliqués against backdrops of cantaloupe-tinged walls.

Blue Woman
Taroudant, Morocco

Painted Door
Tiznit, Morocco

of twisting steps, dark impasses, and leftover spaces are so labyrinthine and dense that the sun cannot be depended upon for direction. Only occasional shafts of burning sunlight pierce the cool darkness. The wave of a breeze, the drone of the *muezzin's* wail, the sound of my footsteps and no others at prayer time, and the odor of *tajine* stews, fresh-cut mint, and chalk are all woven together like a stream of Moroccan music.

The navel of this human warren is the village *souk* (marketplace): a crowded, chaotic, open-air bazaar of miniature shops and stalls. Here crafts are made and goods sold, everything from sheep heads strung with flies, flashing daggers, and mounds of figs to tinsel-stitched ribbon and worn-out European suits. But heaven help me when I need to buy something. Then bartering begins, and I must deal with the consummate dealers. Moroccan merchants are entrepreneurial pit bulls. Merely walking past a shop invites attack. Gesticulating wildly, an assailant drags me into his booth for an exorbitant display of wares and emotions. He jumps up and down with alacrity, earnestly proclaiming the astonishing quality and rarity of his stock, only to evict me for suggesting an unworthy offer. Then I am lured back to be wheedled with mint tea and double-talk. The price of everything from yogurt to hotel rooms to an umbrella in a Fes department store is dependent upon this game of manipulation, contradiction, intimidation, humiliation, exhaustion, and pride.

Reaching Morocco is always a jolt. It is not just the guides, *medinas,* or bargaining. It is that here I am an intruder, wholly apart from local life. I can avoid, affect, or anticipate little and must adapt to alien concepts of time, purpose, and thought. Ambiguity is preferable to precision, and my programmed efficiency is not prized. Cryptic ceremonies, of which I have no clue, are demanded, and ordinary Western manners are to no avail. Attempts are often made to commandeer my camera and clothing upon arrival in a village, for there are few personal rights of ownership. A prolonged period in Morocco without news or communication with anyone who does not see in me a gold mine intensifies my emotions and reactions. Daily existence becomes a comic opera of confusion, magic, beauty, and bewilderment.

A less drastic transition than most is to arrive on the African continent by way of Ceuta, a postage stamp of Spanish territory affixed to the edge of Morocco's Mediterranean coast. From this duty-free port and smuggler's heaven where Spain and Morocco collide, I catch the bus to Tetuán and the alchemy of the East. This short ride always stretches into hours because, several times along the route, police halt the transport to conduct excruciatingly long, choreographed searches of all totes and travelers except for the untouchable, swathed Moroccan females. Near the end of the journey, the driver pulls up to a police way station and pays off the chief in bottles of Spanish whiskey. Then the women, who have stuffed incredible quantities into their amorphous robes, lose hundreds of pounds each as cigarettes, liquor, transistor

From eternally pink Marrakesh and velvety blue Chaouen to green-tiled Meknes and the damask walls of Taroudant, color bears a heavy weight in the architecture and decoration of Morocco. Because strict Islamic tradition bans portrayal of man or animal, representational painting and sculpture never saw a dawn here. Under this taboo Moslems turned to abstracted flowers, tendrils, and rhythmic repetitions of geometry and calligraphy for inspiration. And to make these come alive, color was raised to great importance.

Early use of color can still be seen in the interiors of monuments. There it flourished in vividly glazed tile mosaics, or *zellij,* and on sumptuously painted and gilded spiraling plasterwork and filigree-carved cedar. Woven and folded bands of design evoked the packing straps of nomads, fluid script voiced lessons from the Koran, and tiled fountains recalled oases. The exteriors of mosques and minarets were originally deeply colored as well, their façades faced with plaster, their tiers of decoration boldly painted. But as dynasties fell, pigment and plaster disappeared, exposing plain brick. Today, color traditions are entrusted to the simple village houses where paint is necessary protection from weather and erosion. This is especially true in the South, where infrequent but torrential rains can quickly wash away mud walls without their coat of color.

Unlike much of North Africa, Morocco was little colonized by the Roman Empire and remained in the control of feuding indigenous Berber clans until the arrival of Islam. Just seventy years after the seventh-century Arabian merchant-turned-prophet, Mohammed, transcribed the word of God into the holy Koran, this new religion's cry to prayer rang from minarets along Morocco's Atlantic coast. The converted Berbers—called Moors by Europeans, because they arrived via Morocco, or Roman Mauritania—soon flooded across the Strait of Gibraltar, up through Spain, and as far as the Pyrenees of France, carrying Islam's banner.

As the Dark Ages descended on Christian Europe, Moors became the torchbearers of civilization. Diligently preserving and building upon the knowledge of the ancients, they made great strides in philosophy, science, mathematics, medicine, art, and architecture. Moorish Spain prospered, eclipsing Morocco and even Islam's Mother, Arabia, in culture and luxury. The Renaissance unfolded only as fifteenth-century Europeans traveled to Moslem centers to pore over classical manuscripts and absorb innovations.

As Europe revived, Catholics rallied, chasing Islam back into Morocco. There, in the aftershock of defeat, intellectual curiosity was discouraged; and a distrust of all things foreign descended. For nearly five hundred years the Moors maintained almost total isolation, their once-vital society stagnating. When European powers began to carve Africa into valuable colonies early in this century, Morocco was the most backward country in the entire Mediterranean. Heads of thieves and traitors basking on battlements were very much in vogue, and cities still bolted fast their gates each night in feudal seclusion when France and Spain arrived to divide up the land.

The French believed themselves protectors and the ferriers of cultural benefit to the underdeveloped. The Spanish, on the other hand, approached Morocco in their customary role as conquistadors. So while France left a legacy of language, civilized government, and modern rail and road systems, those regions held by Spain inherited little more than whitewash. In the 1950s, after French-educated Moroccans demanded reform and were ignored, a spiral of escalating violence led to independence. Today, as French and Spanish influences fade, their tenure of ashen gray and dull white tarnish is rubbed away. Each time I return, more evidence of the Berbers' love of color is gloriously unveiled.

When traveling in Morocco, my quest for color battles my instinct for survival. Unlike other areas in which I work, here decisions must often be based on avoiding potential hazards rather than on achieving aesthetic goals. Ever-shifting border wars, locust swarms, and unbearable heat or mountain snow become entangled with the country's standard fare of robust roaches, latent dysentery, unidentifiable foodstuffs, and the mysteries of transportation and language. The greatest challenge to travel, however, is not these inherent hitches but the pestilent, self-appointed "guides." Huge families have given rise to high unemployment in Morocco, and now Allah's former blessing of free family labor has evolved into a plague of roving youth.

"Hello, my friend. Speak English?" are the ominous first words every visitor hears echoing through the convention of teenage boys invariably stationed about the entry of every Moroccan town. When I do not respond, this greeting is pitched aggressively in a dozen languages until finally, in frustration, I fatally confess my tongue. The victor then lays claim to me in the street. With meter running in a highly refined employment-protection-kickback racket, he inserts himself into my itinerary, ever looking for loopholes in the meaning of the word "no." Never to be shaken, only temporarily avoided or defiantly confronted, the "guide" monitors all movement, attempting to drag me to places I do not want to go, while badgering me to buy things I do not want to buy. Like mosquitoes buzzing in the ear, these pesky escorts never stop hovering.

The rationale for this touring service is the difficulty of soloing through Morocco's *medinas*, convoluted old towns where color and tradition triumph. Unhampered by planning, *medinas* defy anyone accustomed to Western organization, street names, and addresses. Tortuous mazes of tumbling, needle-narrow capillaries constantly changing in width, direction, and level, these elaborate, often cloth-covered networks radios, and other illegal or highly taxable goods emerge from beneath their colorful layers; and a party breaks out on board.

The moment we reach Tetuán, I squeeze my way through the hurricane of hustlers who colonize the seedy terminal and onto the next bus leaving for the mountain village of Chaouen. Visions of sand, dry heat, and camels vanish as rain falls on the rickety coach carrying me inland up maniacal switchbacks through the startlingly lush Rif highlands. In every direction cloud-crowned emerald mountains are sculptured with terraces of verdant wheat or cut by swollen streams and falls breaking stands of giant cedar and pine. I remember my first pilgrimage to Chaouen well, for the Rif surrendered the visual keepsake of a young shepherdess carrying a baby, high atop a spur of fractured stone. Wrapped in a sheet of plastic against wind and rain, she was adrift in the black storm, her face a mask of determination as she struggled to attend her flock.

In the heart of this unexpected Eden hides Chaouen, an ancient hill town founded as a haven for Moors escaping the Inquisition. Isolated geographically by mountainous terrain, and socially by its status as a Moslem high-holy site harboring the bones of the Berbers' patron saint, Chaouen denied access to everything Western until the Spanish occupation just sixty years ago. It still retains its customs and an atmosphere of mystery from centuries of seclusion.

Today, Chaouen is a large village of Berber craftsmen and farmers that climbs a hillside at the source of a natural spring. Its stucco-covered brick-and-stone shops and houses are accented with Arabic details, rounded and softened by decades of wear and the buildup of layers of blue-tinted whitewash. When it rains, the color wash deepens in hue, and the town glows an intense blue ranging from pale cerulean to aquamarine. Throughout the Mediterranean the color blue is used as a block against the Evil Eye and bad luck in general, a practice dating from ancient Egypt. In Chaouen it is also believed helpful in keeping mosquitoes and flies at bay.

Preparation of the tinted whitewash, like all Moroccan production, takes place on a tiny scale. Burned limestone, sold by weight in the marketplace, is crushed and then combined with water, flour, salt, and blue pigment derived from copper or cobalt ore. The resulting solution is brushed on the exteriors and throughout the interiors of *medina* homes every year at the end of Ramadan, the month-long ritual daylight fast commemorating the revelation of the Koran to Mohammed.

Five days a week, much of Chaouen life remains hidden behind the blue walls. But on market days, Berbers from the surrounding hills descend on the town and engulf the main square, exchanging local news and bartering what they produce for what they cannot. Then privacy and calm give way to a spectacle reminiscent of a county fair.

Berber Woman
Chaouen, Morocco

Senses are besieged by the smell of sweat and dust, the sting of spices and mint, smoke from wood fires baking bread, animal droppings, overripe vegetables, and the sweet scent of cedar shavings. The usual droning of prayer calls and the clamor of children playing or scolding are augmented by the whining of livestock and screams of their handlers yelling to the thicket, *balek, balek,* make way. Chickens squawk as they are bandied about upside down. Vendors bark above the din of music stalls blaring tapes of Egyptian pop, American country, or sixties rock. A lone government-sponsored nurse expounding on intestinal parasites and rat abatement strains to be heard over the blast of the medicine men's amplified spiels touting passion meters, powders, potions, leeches, and dried lizards.

Donkeys, sheep, and goats thread their way through the yard-wide cobblestone lanes, jostling for right-of-way with bevies of Berber women filled out in their baffling array of candy-striped cottons, gossamer flowered fabrics, and tasseled bath towels—dozens to a body. These bulbous swirls of color and pattern are topped with voluminous straw hats dangling red and blue wool pompons. Carrying tremendous bundles and usually a small child tied to their backs by yet another sparkling shawl, the women conduct the business. They greet one another with a quick handshake, weighty silver bracelets flashing, followed by a kiss to their own hand. Amidst all the labor, sedentary men cluster idly in groups or lounge in cafés sipping mint tea, seemingly without occupation, diversion, or ambition.

One drizzly morning after photographing market activity from my balcony above the busy main square, I wandered through the foggy blue *medina.* A beautiful child of about ten years caught my attention by chattering to me in French, her second language. She assumed that I, a foreigner, would surely understand a foreign tongue, though in fact I grasped little. Curious, energetic, smiling, laughing, she would appear and disappear, leading me up and down the narrow streets. Eventually her game of hide-and-seek took me to an alley alive with color and Eastern ornament. As I set up my camera, it began to rain. I was about to take cover when the shower quieted, and the girl suddenly materialized again, running past me down the blue-traced passage. Later she led me to her home. Opening the deteriorating, iris-blue door set into a decaying rubble wall revealed a fresh, luxuriant inner courtyard hung with vines and paved a checkerboard of black-and-white marble. Answering her shy wave goodbye, I stepped back into the timeless street.

Years passed, and one day I returned to the house with Sally to deliver a print of the photograph to the little girl. We were met at the door by a child who could have been her twin—actually, she was a younger sister. The extended family of mother, brothers, aunt, cousins, grandmother, and in-laws welcomed us into their home with an elaborate puzzle of bobbing and hand kissing, and honored us with Coca-Cola

Street in Chaouen
Morocco

and their friendship. We learned that the girl in the photograph, now seventeen, was living in Belgium, the mother of two and married to her cousin, considered an ideal Arab union. He had stolen her liver, I was told, for Berbers believe this, and not the heart, to be the seat of affection. When they paraded us back to the alleyway, veiled heads popped out of windows, and a large group of neighbors swooped into the street. They excitedly identified their window, their stoop, or their basket in the picture, clapping, buzzing, clicking, chirping, laughing with delight, and insisting they see the photograph and hear the tale.

To the south, along the Atlantic coast, lies Rabat. For a nation's capital, this city is charmingly small and provincial, really just a large village. Its dense old town and arcaded boulevards can make one unique claim, however. They will not doom me to walk as a combatant, continually grappling with guides or exercising my impulse for self-preservation. Because Rabat is the backyard of the king, soldiers keep the city relatively clean, orderly, and cleared of hustlers.

The *medina* of Rabat is thick with color and fragrance. The main artery, leading from the huge fruit and flower *souk* to the cliff-top cemetery, is a continuous chain of stalls and cubicles spattered with fauve awnings and splashed with paint, tile, and stenciled patterns of guardian horns, stars, and crescents. Painted iron doorknockers, in the shape of a downward pointing hand clasping a ball, grace entrances, as they do throughout Morocco and Iberia. This amulet is referred to as the hand of Fátima, after the Prophet's beloved daughter. But this same ornament was used in first-century Pompeii for an identical purpose, long before Islam was born.

I marveled at the thriving dental community. Oral assassins advertised with lurid quantities of used dentures for sale from glass cases displayed beneath shiny portrayals of alluring smiles. Corn was in season during my last visit. Large ears, charcoal burned and sprinkled with spices, were smoking at every turn in the *souk*. The most comical sight I ever witnessed in Morocco was a Rabat curb lined with shrouded women, evidently still in possession of their own teeth, attempting to chomp the kernels daintily. It was an operation calling for three hands, as dashes of bright yellow cob protruded indelicately from either side of their veils.

One afternoon, unhampered by guides, I was free to follow a funeral procession through the *medina*. Chanting, turbaned men held the white-wrapped body aloft on an open, stretcherlike bier. Wailing women trailed in their finest brocade, clasping and unclasping hands in a gesture for what was lost. They soon forgot the corpse and began to screech and warble wildly at the sky. To the beat of drums, we pressed on toward the grave where the departed would recline facing Mecca to await Allah's call.

Bananas
Medina, Rabat, Morocco

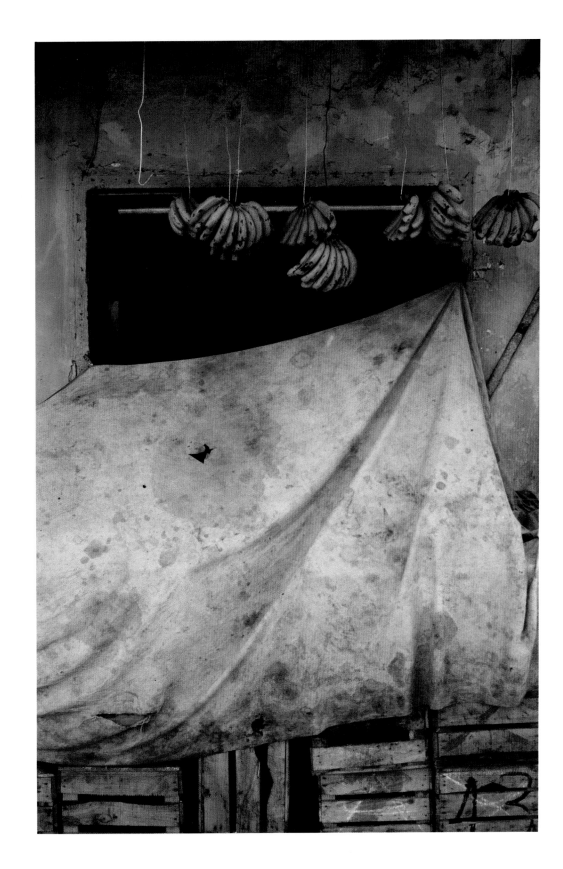

Fátima's Hand
Asilah, Morocco

Well inland and south of Rabat is Marrakesh, the capital of Morocco's spirit. Sprawling, mud-built, salmon pink, and palm-girdled, it is the final outpost of the Mediterranean North and gateway to the Sahara. Hard behind Marrakesh are the sheer, snow-capped High Atlas peaks, yet the town itself summons desert dreams of nomadic caravans and steamy espionage. The city is a little too dense, the guides a little too desperate, and the *medina* a bit too large for me ever to feel at ease here. The crush of life is overwhelming but nonetheless compelling.

To the ringing of hammers on sheets of brass, I make my way to the dyers' domain. Skeins of raw wool float by on the backs of straining donkeys or drip and steam from overhead poles after bubbling in mammoth iron kettles filled with soups of deep indigo, rich crimson from poppies, green from mint, yellow from saffron, and antimony black. Marrakesh hosts the largest *souk* in Morocco, consuming nearly two square miles. Getting lost is inevitable. With troops of befuddled tourists sporting bulging wallets, Marrakesh has become the Mecca for guides, who come to study at her school of sharks.

The student union for this university of guides is a large, dusty square on the edge of the swollen *medina*, the *Djemaa el Fna*, once the site of weekly executions. As evening falls, kerosene lamps attract a churning caldron of Bedouin bag ladies, jugglers, flame eaters, trained monkeys, trance healers, professional penmen, saints, sorcerers, and madmen. Orange-juice squeezers and nut roasters, horse taxis and police work the perimeter. Child boxers take on all comers. Snake charmers weave viperous tunes. Chanting herbalists cast spells with stuffed birds, gazelle horns, dried toads, talons, and mystic concoctions fanned out before them in tin tea cannisters on carpets of violently colored thread. A dentist or two are always on hand, a tray of thousands of unbroken molars attesting to their skill; aching teeth are summarily removed with the aid of lead pipe and pliers. Dancers and musicians twist and swirl amid a cat scream of pipes, jangling tambourines, sawing fiddles, and rattling tall drums. Gamblers perfect their sleight of hand, while soothsayers, conjurers, charlatans, and beggars bleat monotonous mantras.

Mohammed's Revenge caught up with me in the seaside town of Essaouira, due west of Marrakesh. For over a week I was a captive of my room in a hotel washed robin's egg blue, inside and out. Weaving into my consciousness through delirious distress were the daily quintuplet of singsongy summonings to the faithful from the overlapping quartet of neighborhood minarets, marking the passing hours. I began to resent the daybreak cry that awoke me to exhort that prayer is better than sleep.

After a few days the concerned desk clerk, realizing my plight, shared a family recipe: an anomalous brew of Pepsi and goat's milk, heated, shaken, then swilled down in one gulp. Or, if I preferred, he knew of a specialist who could plaster my stomach with an herb-and-flour pack applied with a silver-and-carnelian spatula guaranteed to do the trick. I thanked him but decided to try my luck at the French pharmacy. I should have opted for the home remedy, since the prescription only made things worse. A Peace Corps volunteer assigned to a nearby village informed me, too late, that Westerners simply cannot escape periodic dysentery in Africa but assured me that, untended, it soon retreats.

Once recovered, I found myself in an elegant town embraced by palms and blush-rose crenelated walls. Essaouira is a powerful place, wind-blown and melancholy, with whitewashed, blue-shuttered houses. Pastel robes billowing in the stiff breeze, villagers walk along the sea, past ruins of a sunken castle, toward the massive town gates. Offshore are islands nurturing a rare mollusk that supplied the imperial deep-red dye of Rome. In late afternoon, townswomen, fully enveloped in pistachio, orchid, and powder blue with only tiny slits for navigation, drift about the salt-swept square. The setting sun, reflecting off medieval walls, burnishes these human bundles of cloth gilt pink.

Essaouira's main street is a colonnade of seductive staples, from donkey bridles to harem pants. In the center of the *souk* sits a heap of spice merchants, their counters groaning with unique, aromatic buffets, pungent, piquant, or perfumed. These pyramids of curries and chillies, cinnamon and date sugar, saffron, ginger, turmeric, and coriander satisfy a multitude of dishes, wishes and ills.

The Essaouiran spice seller is also druggist and Avon Lady. So next to his signature seasonings are piles of rock shampoo, lipstick stones, myrrh perfume, crystalline antimony eyeliner, walnut-bark toothbrushes, female cacti-boring insects dried and ground to red powder for rouge, and a rainbow of pigments for eye shadow, sold per application. Green henna for hair and hands is a big draw: the only makeup maidens may use. Applied beauty is often assisted by a vast array of crushed, pulverized, or preserved bits of plants, animals, and minerals believed effective spellbinders; while bright paper fetishes frustrate romantic disaster.

Morocco seethes with a plethora of bus lines offering conflicting (when not mythical) schedules, routes, and fares. Competition is fierce. Well before the challenge of the journey itself comes the Rubik's Cube quest for a carrier. Attempting to reach Agadir, I fumbled my way through the confusion of blue-frocked men, some with and some only feigning knowledge and authority. I eventually placed my bet and sat waiting on an overturned bucket in the Essaouira station, a series of sheet-metal huts located just outside the town walls among the swarm of shills lying in ambush for the next hapless traveler.

My bus arrived in a swirl of dust and diesel fumes, its engine revving wildly. In a flurry of activity, bags, boxes, a bicycle, and one revered retread were compelled

Spice Seller's Wall
Essaouira, Morocco

onto the netted mountain of goods capping the Methuselan rattletrap. To the refrain "Agadiragadiragadiragadir," passengers piled on; the conductor, riding shotgun, slammed the door; and we jerked and shuddered southward. At any opportunity and every official stop, aspiring musicians, mendicants, and cripples with bodily horrors hopped aboard to soliloquize on hard luck. After a few *dirhams* had passed their way, they exited, and we hobbled on. Midway, everyone's attention was distracted from the hairpin turns by my seatmates' argument, escalating to near homicide, over some rabbits drugged for ease of transport staring glassy-eyed from the overhead rack. Seasoned riders brought lemons to suck to steady the dizzying route, but motion sickness took its toll on babies and old folk. By the time we reached Agadir seven hours later, my traumatized companions and I felt as bad as the crate of wind-plucked chickens recovered from high atop the craft.

Agadir, toppled by an earthquake in 1960, slid downhill, metamorphosing during reconstruction into an Atlantic resort. Tourism at its most tepid, this new Agadir is a sterile slice of northern Europe with winter sun, severed entirely from anything genuinely Moroccan. The few guides wander aimlessly. Counterfeit nomads sell paste jewelry or stage whimsical camel races on the beach. Bogus belly dancers provide glaringly inauthentic entertainment in upholstered indoor tents at overblown Arabian feasts. Occasionally I have seen a Blue Moor of the Sahara, still robed and veiled against sandstorms in layers of indigo cheesecloth, wander in off the desert to perform complete ablutions in a café washroom. He and his ship of the desert drop anchor, looking lost among the broad, paved avenues—incognito among the imitations.

Southeast of Agadir in the Anti-Atlas Mountains, villagers are self-sufficient and rarely leave their homes, so public transportation is severely pruned. An automobile is the only reasonable way to reach this remote country. I always secure my rental car in Agadir, thankfully without the convoluted bartering system of real Morocco or the intercession of guides. With so few vehicles traversing this region, the roads are in uncannily perfect condition. It can be hours between passing another car or even a tail-swishing haystack moving on donkey legs.

Color abruptly returns to architecture upon escaping the confines of the district of Agadir. To the north are the color-washed houses of Tarhazoute. More startling, in the monochrome landscape on the road east to Taroudant, there is a line of demarcation drawn precisely at the sign announcing the new province. On one side all is whitewash or unpainted clay, punctuated only by the outline of high-domed saints' tombs and ziggurat-topped towers. Just across the road, every mud-daubed shelter is suddenly red as a fez, banana yellow, Persian blue, or kiwi green, with shutters and doors striped, dotted, and chevroned in a wild array of hues.

Straw Wall
Hafaya, Morocco

Fishing Nets
Agadir, Morocco

Fishing Boat
Tarhazoute, Morocco

Taroudant is a blast of heat completely enclosed by majestic, tomato red, crenelated walls of baked mud twenty feet high. Women in brilliant costume move against the ramparts looking like tropical fish swimming in a red sea. In the 115-degree heat, Sally and I had decided to wear shorts, inviting onslaught. The moment we emerged from the car, the ubiquitous "Mohammed" latched on. I had learned long ago that if I retained a young enough scout, he was too impressed by my age and size to attempt to control my destinations but could still prove valuable for keeping older leeches at bay. This Mohammed fit the bill, and besides, it was too hot for evasive tactics. He was thoroughly confounded by our lack of interest in Taroudant's carpet showrooms or any of the other goals on his agenda. And he was more than a little disappointed by my interest in the plain, painted houses as he realized this would net him no clandestine commissions.

At lunchtime he led us to a tiny restaurant where chick-pea soup was simmering in what looked to be a fifty-gallon oil drum in back. The "chef" smiled with delight at the foreign patronage. Joining us at a listing table flecked with ceiling plaster, little Mohammed valiantly attempted to answer my unorthodox questions about color, paint, and traditions as best he could, fleshing out the walls with preposterously unhistorical though inspired replies.

Just as I was about to reward our friend for his imagination and the tasty bargain meal, the police drove up in a jeep, entered the establishment, and snatched him into custody. Guides are illegal throughout Morocco, but only in Rabat or a small village like Taroudant can the restriction be enforced. The officers apologized profusely in French, emphasizing that Mohammed was a repeat offender. Terrified, our ex-escort was carried off, feet dragging in the dust, despite our best efforts on his behalf.

Without a guide, for all potentials had been scared into passivity by word of the arrest, I was easily able to survey the rest of the town. Many of the houses in Taroudant are decorated with crushed colored glass from broken bottles mixed with mortar. This forms a kind of gaudy exposed aggregate, which is set into walls in designs meant to ward off calamity or cultivate happiness. The richness of the ornament is typical of the outer flamboyance found in southern Morocco, which is rare in the more introverted North.

While I continued working one evening, Sally joined the double-dyed farm wives gossiping just inside the city gate. Without intention of profit, Moroccan women warm to one out of genuine curiosity. The covey gathered around Sally and let down their veils to whisper or point, smile and giggle, as they mimed questions about marriage and children, husband and home. There seemed to be no middle age among them; with masks removed they were either adolescent or prematurely gray. Women

Shop Wall
Taroudant, Morocco

bank their wealth in silver and gold, worn as solid armor and usually locked in brilliant layers of cloth. They showed her pounds of bracelets on organdy-bound wrists and ankles, and gilded horns, hands, and hearts to enchant, protect, and prosper. Studying her bare legs, sandals, and lack of jewelry, they must have assumed Sally was either poor or star-crossed, and badly in need of charms.

We wondered about our young guide. Was he rotting in prison because of me? I asked the restaurateur and others to whom we had been introduced, but no one could say, only that it was Allah's will. Then one evening Mohammed appeared on a lame bicycle. Brushing off the incident in his joy at finding us before our departure, he sheepishly hinted that his tip was overdue.

Driving farther south, I know I have reached a town, even if there is no evidence of houses or people, when I pass under gigantic, brightly painted ceremonial arches that mark village limits. Suddenly, these elaborate triumphal concrete sculptures appear, looming carnation pink, green, and turquoise, pockmarked with stars and crescents, and waving flags, banners, and sometimes a large, sun-bleached poster of the smiling king. Introduced by the French as a kind of militaristic flourish, this architectural extravagance has persisted. Often the arches are the only sign of vitality in a settlement that otherwise exists solely on market day, when outlying farmers swarm to the crossroads to barter. The rest of the time a lonely skeleton of stalls remains, brightly painted and sandblasted, shutters banging in the wind, awaiting rebirth.

Many of these "villages" support only a café or trading post where travelers can buy a warm soda, maybe some gas, but little else. When I stop, inquisitive children appear out of nowhere to hop alongside the car like puppies, giggling and pointing for a *dirham* coin or a sweet. "Monsieur-Madame" is called out to me in mimicked confusion. Sometimes the kids just stare intently, as if I were a Martian. Little girls with hennaed hair, torn between fear and the desire to touch my camera, scurry back and forth, clinging to one another and shrieking with laughter.

Before the veil, both boys and girls run wild together; only later do women swaddle and hide. Seclusion is not a part of Islam; it was established later, partly to preserve morality but also to conceal beautiful faces from admiration, which could attract the dreaded Evil Eye. Ancient fears are also mostly responsible for the reluctance of women to be photographed. They believe that anything personal, even a name or shadow, can imperil their lives if it falls into malevolent hands. This holds for their image as well; so they will seldom release it to a stranger.

At one road stop I photographed a painted clock, its hands frozen forever at the midday hour of submission. A little boy took my hand, touched it to his chest, forehead, and lips in salutation, then led me inside his home to show off an antique timepiece from Germany. Clocks are a proud possession in this land where they guard the precious knowledge of accurate prayer times. Only after I had recorded the family heirloom was he satisfied.

My tinny Renault bumped and strained through heat-hazed Anti-Atlas passes. Yellow wind whipped across the pre-Saharan wasteland of stone, stubble, and sand, as vultures wheeled between fractured peaks. By midday the air was scorching. I could hear my tires peeling tar from the road. After hours in this vacuum, the faint image of a camel driver floated out of a distant, shivering rock. Where could he live in this inhospitable dominion of sun and gravel? From time to time scruffy argan trees offered juicy leaves to tree-climbing goats, who balanced on the weak limbs like silly characters from Dr. Seuss. Or I would spot a solitary shepherd, his flock a whirl of dust. Then I knew a bone-dry village radiating paths to nowhere would soon appear, trapped in the cliffs or silhouetted against the pale turquoise, sand-dimmed sky.

Eventually I reached a crossroads' luminous landmark of polychrome striped cloth. It was a drift of hitchhiking Berbers with bundles and staves squatting for what might have been days in hope of a ride. A boulder scrawled with yellow and red chalk arrows targeted five divergent directions, each identified in Arabic script. As I strained to translate the graffiti, one smiling applicant with a polished charcoal face and pineapple-patterned shirt underneath a lavender *djellaba* explained that the group was off to Marrakesh for promised work. But they had come from Tafraoute, and he pointed the way. By late afternoon I was descending into a valley of almond orchards, where small tended plots of terraced land crowded billowing sandstone cliffs pasted with crenelated kasbahs. The still air was heavy. Tangerine-tinted light irradiated the chunks of pink granite absurdly stacked about the wind-eroded, palm-studded landscape.

My Tafraoute hotel was a Hollywood facsimile of a Foreign Legion fort overlooking this dinosaur-movie set. I longed for a swim, but the promised pool was a decoy, a cracked sea-green basin empty for a decade. Following suit, the rooms had no hot water before sunset and no electricity after. I collapsed from heat into the huge bed and awoke to French jazz emanating from an ancient Victrola in the courtyard. Opening the eight-foot-high shutters, I saw desert dusk turn to Arabian night. An orange rind, topped with pale aqua and edged in persimmon pink at the horizon, grew thick with blazing stars as the jagged Atlas bloomed deep violet.

Each day, in the cool of approaching dawn, I hiked past bright green prickly pear goat corrals and girls drawing water from wells on my way to the scattered gingerbread *ksar* hiding among the boulders. These fortress-villages with thick walls and tapering towers are built of *tabia*, a native concrete of lime and pebbles or

Shuttered Window
Tafraoute, Morocco

straw mixed with earth, ranging in color from dahlia red to honey. The sloping walls, projecting rainspouts, palm-wood doors, and palm-frond-molded window slits are often embellished with brilliant paint accentuating incised incantations of circles, stars, hands, crescents, ziggurats, dots, and dashes. When arranged in vertical patterns, these give the impression of soaring height.

A face-lift of rebuilding and repainting village walls that have been melted by winter rain is accomplished before the annual *moussem*, or festival honoring the local saint. Rural Berbers still place great trust in their *marabouts*, most of whom lived lives more fierce and powerful than holy. Endowed with *baraka* (mystical powers), these venerated figures inspire pilgrimage and celebration; some became the center of fanatical, violent cults. Members of certain brotherhoods were renowned for fire walking, trance healing, levitation, and devouring live snakes, scorpions, sheep, and goats, as well as various frenzied acts of self-mutilation. While these extreme activities have been banned by both French and Moroccan governments, the fraternities still thrive among the Berber tribes. One day, as I approached a sacred tomb, I came upon a tree tied with brightly colored rags. I learned that these villagers believe that if a cloth is rubbed on an ailing body part and placed near the saint, the illness is absorbed.

South of Tafraoute, as far east as Algeria, occasional oases astonish one by sprouting up out of the blue-white glare in the thirsty Anti-Atlas. Pre-Saharan life is confined to these narrow ribbons of fertile land, with their oceans of date palms following capricious underground rivers. Here, fortified stone or mud *ksars* form natural extensions of the bands of cold mineral-green copper, rust-red iron ore, yellow sandstone, chalky white limestone, dull purple basalt, and lime-green gypsum striping the desert cliffs. Built and rebuilt on a similar plan through the centuries to protect and exploit the now-vanished caravans with their cargoes of gold, slaves, ivory, and salt, the *ksars* of the oases are today without purpose, their inhabitants without future. The dwindling Berbers who do hold on maintain virtually complete independence, refusing government taxation, services, or control—holdovers from days when the lords of the Atlas reigned. There is no concept of antique here. Everything is old. And old can mean thirty years or thirty centuries. After millennia of existence, when the occasional downpour arrives, villages fall to ruin or melt back into the earth, never to be resurrected.

Heading toward Tan-Tan, I was frequently stopped at police checkpoints and by soldiers on maneuvers near the endlessly disputed border with Mauritania. Roads that degenerated into faint trails marked only by pyramids of black stones or the bones of camels, trucks, and tanks that had died along the way finally convinced me to turn back toward Tiznit.

Kasbah
Tafraoute, Morocco

Farm Wall
Tafraoute, Morocco

Hand
Tiznit, Morocco

Founded in this century as a frontier outpost, Tiznit may be new, but life continues much as it had in biblical times. Inside its *medina,* sand blasts rip through the grid of streets, always reminding one of the desert's grasp. In Tiznit both paint and symbol combine on every doorway, façade, and element of stucco or caked mud in a full-blown, magical barrage against demons and bad luck. This village is the quintessential example of the use of vernacular color and sign. Hands, eyes, crescent moons, five-pointed stars, horseshoes, curved horns, fish, hearts, bells, iron studs, colorful ribbons, and brilliant birds' feathers, drawn on or nailed to the houses, together with generously and imaginatively applied paint, form a powerful battery to thwart *el-Ain,* the Evil Eye. Throughout the Mediterranean there is the widely held belief that by attracting the Evil Eye's most virulent first glance to something striking, whether colorful, fortunately shaped, or musical, its force can be baffled, distracted, or exhausted before reaching inside a house for a victim.

All of these symbols can be traced back at least thirty centuries, through pagan, Christian, and Islamic cultures. The crescent, among the most prevalent, is derived from the Egyptian fertility goddess, Isis, who was always portrayed with an upturned crescent moon over her head. Through Greek and Roman civilizations, the crescent form and anything of similar shape, including cow horns, arched doorways, and horseshoes, were used to invoke the favor of this powerful goddess and protect against evil. The crescent arch of so many of Tiznit's doorways is reinforced by stepped surrounds of vivid hues to emphasize the lucky contour. Horseshoes are thought doubly potent in Morocco because iron here is considered a vigorous demon-chaser. The open hand has perhaps even more ancient roots. When Islam arrived, these pagan symbols were incorporated, even when their image ran afoul of the strict Islamic ban on representation. Today, many Tiznit houses sport large, upright hands and eyes embossed upon the keystones of their entry arches in an ancient tradition that has overpowered religious dogma.

But mostly it is the variety and boldness of the colors that the villagers rely on to scare away misfortune. One morning I watched a man confidently painting his shop an auspicious, buoyant blue. Even I thought it looked reassuring, something like the shade at the bottom of a swimming pool. With a long-handled, round-bristle brush, he slapped on the paint. After splashing saturated pink across his counter, he stenciled rows of Nile-green hands and lemon-yellow stars around his door until he was sure to be safe and prosperous, surrounded by his fresh bouquet of color.

Decorated Door
Tiznit, Morocco

Greece

Iris, goddess of the rainbow, gowned in radiant spectrum, was on hand for the birth of Greece—and so were her colors. Mythology reserved an exalted position for this beloved creator of *chromata*, for although blinding white is the common perception of the country today, Greece has a tradition of painted color unfulfilled by the present pallor. Her celebrated classical ruins of pristine white marble are just the bleached bones of a culture once saturated with pigment.

Drawing on myths of the pharaohs, ancient Hellenes devised an Olympian world in which gods were granted individual powers and identified with specific colors. The red of blood and fire eventually came to be associated with war, birth, sacrifice, and the soul. The blue of the sky spoke of truth and the ascendency of the spiritual realm over evil, while the green of spring expressed youth, beauty, love, and healing. Buildings both modest and magnificent paraded these symbolic shades to invoke favor. By the time of Pericles, temples and palaces were anointed in vivid hues, houses lavishly frescoed, and statues portrayed realistically in natural tones and then robed and rouged to mimic life more closely. The impact must have been far more exuberant and accessible than the austere, formal, godlike presence the relics now embody.

As the sun of the Golden Age set, Imperial Rome, enamored of everything classically Greek, absorbed her gods, architecture, and colors. With the expansion

Copper Cloud
Vathi, Kalymnos, Greece

Faded Paint
Skala, Patmos,
Greece

Singer Wall
Corfu, Greece

of the empire, allegorical color was sown throughout the Mediterranean. There it was left to twist and twine, long after the fall of Rome, bearing new fruit when grafted onto assorted cultures and religions.

With the rise of Christianity, painted pagan temples were abandoned. Greek color, however, lived on in iconic mosaics and frescoes through eleven centuries of Byzantine rule, only to wither when Turks overran Constantinople. Disdainful of Greek heritage and Orthodoxy, the Moslem conquerors cheerfully watched as the Greek birthright was carted off or fell to ruin. Plaster crumbled and paint flaked from carved marble. Gradually, chalky white became the standard for Greece, eventually dominating even humble dwellings.

As the Renaissance blossomed, the focus of intellectual and artistic life returned to Italy. In an attempt to reclaim classical splendor, Italians once again crossed the Ionian to pillage, study, and copy at the source. But nearly two thousand years had passed since the crest of Greek glory, and this time they arrived too late to see the color. So, in erroneous imitation, and against the Italian grain, Greek monuments and sculpture were recreated in stark white marble, stripped of Iris' rainbow.

Fortunately, there are always exceptions to any rule in architecture, and so it is with the hoary white of modern Greece. In vernacular buildings these anomalies take several forms. The isles nearest to Italy tilt their heads in that direction, and color naturally follows. In the far reaches of the Aegean, the Dodecanese chain sweeps toward Asia Minor, where an Eastern prism shines. And everywhere there is Greek blue, the color of the flag, of striped cloth and shutters, of chapel domes and painted boats. Always abundantly pigmented, this is the shade of the omnipresent sea and cloudless sky, which loom large in the life of this land.

Lying between mainland Greece and southern Italy, the island of Corfu is a bridge over which armies and ideas have always coursed. Color whispers in hundreds of hot little villages scattered across this hilly isle, telling of long-entangled ties with Italy as well as escape from Ottoman dominion. Crawling with bright green lizards, these quiet hamlets crumble, the victims of migration to Athens or abroad. Since tourists have not yet climbed their way up from the beaches to these hidden mountain retreats, customs and traditions survive, just as they have through every other occupation of the island.

Even the most remote village is serviced sporadically by a battered local bus, its windshield garnished with so many safeguards to intimidate road hazards that the driver's view is obscured: a garland of Greek flags and shedding peacock plumes flutter beside hallowed plastic baubles; sequined froufrou dangle beside an electrified icon glowing well-being from the dash. When no bus appears, I travel pungent donkey paths, thick with weeds, or narrow lanes enclosed by low stone walls. Sheets of lavender wildflowers and gnarled olives blanket hills terraced and turned until the land itself looks like hand embroidery. At harvest time these groves are wall-to-wall rag rugs catching the yield, while old women sit on the ground before water troughs sorting the black fruit.

Invariably one dusty road winds past a simple church and belfry, ornament painted sulfur yellow in lieu of gilding. A phalanx of chickens freeze, then squawk and scatter as I approach the cluster of stone and stucco tile-roofed houses. Façades are patinaed in creamy azure, hyacinth, and apple green, with sash, sill, and entry wreathed in a flourish of Italianate plaster touched in pumpkin and mulberry. Garish beads or strips of plastic rustle in open doorways, spurning sun and flies. The café and fruit vendor display beautiful hand-painted signs, and the air tastes of charcoal, lamb, bay leaf, and goat cheese.

Village life distills down to a series of familiar icons. A baggy-trousered, white-haired Byzantine saint licks a dripping orange popsicle. Songbirds sing in the shade of painted cages bookended by geraniums sprouting from olive oil tins. A grandmother with wrinkled, muttering lips cards wool, pinching and twisting it into yarn from a tuft of cotton candy. Sagging wooden porches hold a pedal-driven sewing machine and a greedy goat, tethered for milking. A stooped farmer, the color of worn rock, cuts an arc of brown bread, drawing the knife toward his chest. And women garbed in black bend to gather dinner greens by the side of every road.

One summer in Corfu Town, to elude the searing grasp of the midday sun, Sally and I ducked into the cool eclipse of Saint Spiridon's Church. We watched the smoky icons watching us with their stern, unblinking eyes through a dusky haze of golden light. The narrow aisles were littered with pilgrims crossing themselves, kneeling with stiffly outstretched arms, or echoing poses of the painted saints. Others tucked written desires into the images' silver surrounds rubbed smooth by generations of polishing.

Judging from bedrolls and varied costume, they must have embarked from all the ports of Greece to implore their country's patron saint for assistance. Solid, broad-hipped women rummaged through straw baskets and hushed squealing babies. Mustachioed men with calloused hands and sun-leathered faces seemed out of place, spruced up in scratchy black suits. Their murmurings rose and fell like an ocean tide punctuated by smacking lips kissing the icons. Beeswax candles hissed and spat, their smoke swirling upward with spicy incense, only to be trapped with whispered prayers in the upper recesses of the dome.

We wove our way through the muffled hum and up some steps into a tiny room in the apse, where the ceiling was hung with *tamatas*. Sailing ships, eyes, and curlicued hearts wrought of silver and gold, these votives put silent petition into visual form, though many were destined to be melted down to add more glory to the icons. A great chased silver sarcophagus took up most of the space. We were alone until a stout, determined-looking farm wife, escorted by friends and family, entered with her young crippled daughter in arms. A crowd of bearded priests in dark uniform followed right on their heels. Before we could react, the massive door was shut with a thud and locked with an old-fashioned key.

The air grew chokingly thick with incense. Smoking oil lamps barely caught a gleam from silver halos of frescoed icons on the walls, blackened by centuries of holy soot. As the mysterious ceremony proceeded, the chanting crescendoed. Feeling like intruders, we pressed ourselves into a back corner. A priest unlocked the silver coffin, revealing a glass-encased nightmare: the shriveled, gray face of Saint Spiridon the Miracle Worker. Fourth-century shepherd-turned-bishop, Spiro gets credit for everything good that comes Corfu's way, from mundane miraculous healings and a resurrection to saving the island from famine, plague, Turks, and even World War II German troops. I silently wondered if he were up to today's task.

Shadows leaned to kiss the smudged crystal over the mummy. All attention focused on the terrified child. The priest mumbled some words and crossed the girl's forehead with his thumb. Her mother cried. And then it was over, as quickly as it had begun. The coffin was closed and secured, the door swung open, and we were all released into a rush of cool air. The Age of Miracles revived.

On my last pass through Athens, the city was in the throes of an enervating heat wave. Jammed with immigrants searching for work and masochistic tourists doing the museums, the blistering capital was a sweaty chaos of concrete, tempers, and traffic, all suffocating under a shroud of smog. I waited day after day for a boat with deck space to the islands and their promise of sea breeze and swimming.

Athens never cooled. What little color the city might have offered was drained away by the incandescent sun, which blazed into the asphalt all day only to radiate back as lightless heat throughout the night. The evening *volta* (stroll) was abandoned in the 120-degree temperatures. Shops simply did not reopen. Only puffy-faced lottery vendors kept to their duty, stumbling the white-hot streets, dripping with bandoliers of sticky tickets. Athenians carried aluminum folding lawn chairs to the city park in search of relief. But the refuge was a steamy, insect-ridden dust bowl shrieking with cicadae where wilting geese drooped at the edge of their foul pond in the scant shadow of heat-stressed trees. Dazed residents near collapse still roamed the streets at 3:00 A.M.

When the weekly boat to Patmos docked, I was finally able to escape into the Aegean. The ferry steamed for hours past islands, which randomly rise and fall in popularity and prosperity, much to the bewilderment of natives. Their snow-white cubes and domes, short on rooms, water, and tradition, bristle with rusting rebars thrusting expectantly toward the next floor in hope of an economic upswing.

I was awakened in the middle of the night by shouts and the grinding sound of a monstrous chain being dragged up through the hull. From deck the lights of the mountaintop monastery and its village looked like a low-lying constellation. Dust, desert herbs, sun-baked stone, and threshed wheat—the smells of archaeology— overpowered the darkness.

Serene, mystical, and tradition-bound, the isle of Patmos retains the qualities that compel my return, even though painted color here is subtle, hiding in the harbor or glowing softly among the stone and whitewash. In the tangled mass of Chora, which spills around the monks's home, wind whistles down stepped passages past chipped and faded butter-yellow doors and moss-green shutters overlooking the sea far below.

It was in a cave on this parched pile of rubble jutting out of the sea that the banished Apostle John received the Book of the Revelation when God roared at him through a crack in the stone. Abandoned to rampaging pirates, the island passed a thousand years before the heavy polygonal fortress of a monastery arose. For centuries after, monks were the island's only occupants. They still possess and preside over much of the property, and under their gaze, little changes. Residents continue to cross themselves when passing the Cave of the Apocalypse or any of the hundreds of chapels scattered about the barren hillsides. And the priests, closely linked to daily life, have kept commercialism at bay. Recently, however, pressure has been applied by islanders longing to cash in on tourism, and now music bars and nude sun bathers on the monastery ramparts cloud the horizon.

One April I lingered almost every afternoon watching a shipwright transform a rough-hewn tree into the hull of a fishing trawler. An exquisite skeleton slowly emerged from a hill of shavings. I shared my view of the craftsman's progress with an ancient match seller, whose bright blue shop, the dimensions of a telephone booth, stood in the shadow of the boat ribs. Nearly ninety and almost blind, he was also the island's sign painter and resident artist. His spare hours were spent laboring

Red Anchor
Patmos, Greece

over portraits of boats rendered as flat as the shipyard-scavenged tin on which they were painted.

Thin and frail, he looked even more so in his voluminous black pants, oversized white shirt buttoned to the collar, loose wool vest, and thick-lensed eyeglasses held together with a rubber band. As the weeks went by, he imparted the secrets of his paint box and stories of his life while dispensing wooden matches through a tiny glass window. Spring turned to summer. His health failed, and then one day he died, too soon to see the launching of the ship, enameled in a blazing tribute, the colors he had suggested: Chinese red, zinc yellow, and Prussian blue.

I had been working on Karpathos, a solitary island pounded by the rough seas between Rhodes and Crete. After spending a week in the mountain-locked village of Olymbos studying the carved plasterwork and crude false marbling on the pastel houses, I hiked down through a long, dry valley to the Mediterranean. Reaching the port, I learned that the only passage to my next destination was a livestock freighter to be anchored offshore late that night.

The atmosphere was cold and greasy with dampness from the sea as I huddled on the unsteady wooden pier at midnight. I was relieved when a family joined me. They were laden with years of possessions, including three obstreperous goats. At the blast of a horn, a weary fisherman somehow managed to row our menagerie through black, wind-chopped water to the waiting rust bucket. As we bobbed recklessly alongside, beefy arms extended from a hole in the stern to haul us all in. I tossed up my bag and suddenly found myself aboard. Fierce winds stirred the sea, and the hold full of sheep bleated their displeasure throughout the voyage. At long last I was deposited on Kalymnos the following evening, the only two-footed passenger to disembark.

Kalymnos is an island of sponge divers and purple granite mountains hugging the Turkish coast. Cascading down steep cliffs surrounding the lively port of Pothea are small stucco houses flooded with rich, heavy pigment, staining the harbor with their reflection. Because the island is off the tourist route, however, few realize that Greece holds a native architecture brimming over with painted color.

It was the eve of an island festival, and I had been warned that rooms would be scarce. A scrawny, ill-kept woman met me at the dock trumpeting a private room in her home. While families renting rooms for extra income are common throughout Greece, I was skeptical of my good fortune and her lavish description. But in desperate need of sleep, I was persuaded to accompany her. I wondered which of her children

Grandmother's House
Olymbos, Karpathos, Greece

would be uprooted for my sake. After a twisting ascent past houses screaming their colors, we reached a neoclassical mansion in grave need of repair and paint.

She prodded me through a maze of muggy, high-ceilinged rooms strewn with luggage and sagging beds. Fevered guests drooped in every nook and cranny. Walls were puzzlingly papered with framed photographs and newsprint clippings of some royal family, which she acknowledged reverently while mumbling continuously about a king. Up the creaking staircase of her makeshift boardinghouse, my suspicions were confirmed. This was no ordinary *dhomatia.* The landlady was loony, and my "private room with balcony" was a jumble of cots that had been rented to eight others as well.

When I wheeled around to leave, she counteroffered a mat in the cool outdoor courtyard, neglecting to inform me of her intention to sleep outside as well, after renting out her own bedroom. She snored like a charging rhinoceros. After a sleepless night, I joined the mob milling outside the lone shower. Before I got my turn, a delegation of outraged neighbors, weary of noise and backed-up plumbing on the block, arrived with police in tow. But the mistress of the manor was gone, off to meet the next ship and new recruits, for no one ever stayed longer than one night in her torture chambers.

I learned from a fellow inmate, a Greek who spoke English, that the woman had an altogether unhealthy obsession with the long-deposed king of Greece. Using her unlicensed hotel to finance annual pilgrimages to London, she lived for brief audiences with the exiled monarch.

On my way to new quarters, I watched Pothea slowly break into color through a silver mist. With the passing days, the rhythm of the village made itself apparent. In the mornings, café owners unstacked dawn-damp chairs, and the first patrons sipped coffees. They were soon replaced by a frieze of old men in dark suits and broad-brimmed hats who managed the ever-restless harbor from their favorite quayside seats. After the noontime meal, all of Kalymnos went to sleep. Only in late afternoons did life begin again. Dozing shopkeepers roused themselves to raise shutters. *Tavernas* cranked up the volume on Eastern-flavored melodies broadcast from loudspeakers tacked above their doorways. The music was combated by countertop televisions blaring storms of electronic snow. Oblivious regulars pursued their favorite pastime, arguing over politics like UN delegates, as children darted beneath tables. In the evenings, pedestrians paraded along the waterfront. Restaurateurs presided over trays of moussaka and strings of octopuses, tentacles drooping, while grilled chickens sang with clusters of bees.

Color is the most dramatic feature of Kalymnos life. Each house, poor or prosperous, and every shop, shutter, doorway, and even the streets here are painted with

inspired gusto. Walking through town, I always feel like a trespasser. Concerned islanders constantly ask if I am lost, for few strangers climb the steep, stepped streets to these brightly painted neighborhoods. Family furniture, washtubs, braziers, and activities spill out into any widening. Doors are always open, with the bedroom just a little more closed and protected, just a bit less public than the road. The streets, really paths following the contour of the mountain, become the responsibility and therefore the property of the person who maintains them with broom and paint bucket. Persnickety housewives paint or retouch practically every week, especially in more trafficked courtyards and lanes where wear and dirt threaten.

Walls, built of local porous stone, absorb water; so they must be plastered and painted for protection. But the imaginative colors represent a continuing tradition of lively self-expression. Fresh color often reflects emotions and is especially in evidence on the occasion of births, marriages, reunions, and the approach of great festivals. I was told that a widow paints the surrounds of her door and windows gray for the period of mourning. And I spoke with a mother slathering on peach and parrot green with obvious delight in honor of her daughter's homecoming from America. Once I noticed a house whose window grill was strung with brightly colored yarn. A boy playing outside said it would help his sick sister. The family's talisman reminded me that rural Greece is still a robust alloy of folklore, superstition, and Orthodoxy, where color has meaning deep beneath the surface.

The interiors of homes are also brilliantly painted and individualized, the chromatic walls a backdrop for heirlooms. There is always a lamp burning beneath the family icon, and rows of fragile, hand-tinted wedding photographs or portraits of stoically posed grandfathers in archaic uniform with big, drooping mustaches. Shelves and plate racks are laden with a rainbow of hand-painted ceramics, and all other surfaces are draped with woven and embroidered linens, part of the bridal dowry. But store-bought gizmos, nonsensical trinkets, and the radio receive the most prominent display, testament to the value of mass-produced gadgets over hand labor.

While the Dodecanese Islands, from Patmos and Kalymnos to Rhodes and Karpathos, vary widely in their range and use of color, they are still the most brilliantly painted in all of Greece. Since they span the Ottoman coast, it is probable that color traditions on Kalymnos are partly derived from Eastern influence. Ironically, at least from what I have seen, painted color in Turkey's capital has been lost to a kooky tax strategy in which levies are based upon how a building looks from the street. As this revenue system was explained to me, the snazzier the house appears, the more the owner pays, a detriment both to traditional color and structural stability. For generations the stone and wood of Istanbul have been left to peel or buckle, with hardly a fleck of paint now remaining.

Another story I was told ties Kalymnos color to an act of irascible rebellion against Turkish and Italian occupations. Brilliant Helles blue, associated with patriotism and the Greek homeland, was applied as an exasperating but unpunishable forum for demonstrating discontent: the painted house as provocateur. Over the years the use of color evolved, and Kalymnos is now a riot of invention. Original and daring combinations abound. But Greek blue still reigns, in union with every variation on aqua and plum to harmonize with the color of sea and sky.

Evening Sky
Patmos, Greece

Acknowledgments

To live as a working artist is a dream come true. I know this ideal could never have become reality for me without the love and unquestioning support and encouragement of my parents, William and Jacquelyn Becom, who never pointed out the impractical side of my aspiration.

It has been many years since my second-grade schoolteacher, Mrs. Rohm, allowed me to escape from class recitals on the sweet-potato whistle to the back corner and crayola drawings of Spanish galleons. But the joy of those lost hours in a world of history, art, and faraway lands spurred my imagination. The lessons and zest of Hetty Tucker, Shelby County's beloved regional painter, have also endured. I also acknowledge Roland Hobart, who taught me the basics of abstract design and whose influence I still feel today in my photography. And very important to me during my first, lean years as an artist was the faith and finance of San Francisco attorney and friend Norman Laboe, who always found a bare spot on his wall when I was low on funds.

Mediterranean Color would not have been possible without the tremendous enthusiasm of my Manhattan mentors, Marion and Roger Swaybill, who championed the project and brought all of the participants together. To them, my heartfelt gratitude. I also appreciate the guidance, flexibility, and encouragement of Robert Abrams, Mark Magowan, Alan Axelrod, and Jim Wageman of Abbeville Press during this, my first book and first attempt at writing. I am honored by the involvement of Paul Goldberger, whose interest and participation in the project has been a tremendously satisfying bonus.

My sincere thanks also go to artists Frances and Morley Baer of Carmel for their inspiration, and for their kind assistance in unraveling the mysteries of publishing and galleries; designer Emily Novak and architect George Miers for their confidence in my work and for the early opportunities they provided me; and Carol Williams Christopher, David Stroud, Lauren Deerfield St. Pierre, and the staff of Photography West Gallery in Carmel for all their efforts on my behalf as well as for providing me with the special opportunity to be associated with the legends of photography at this early point in my career.

I applaud the skill and care of Linda Potts, Paul Mason, Pegeen Jones, David Azose, and Esse Carol Anderson Lyle, who have all assisted in preparing the images for this book. I praise the patient, critical eyes of Heidi Aberg Long and Jerry Long, who pored over drafts and rewrites, and the wit and wisdom of David "Hold the Mustard" Jouris, who assisted in the eleventh hour. I also greatly appreciate attorney Roger L. Meredith's kind support and sage advice. And Susan Aberg deserves cheers for her vigilance during my long absences.

I tip my hat to those writers who have been most helpful in guiding my routes and research and verifying legend: Norman F. Carver, Jr., for his illuminating series on Mediterranean hill towns; the old master, H. V. Morton, for his eccentric volumes on Spain and Italy; Edward Allen's *Stone Shelters,* about traditional Apulian buildings; as well as Frederick Thomas Elworthy's 1895 treatise, *The Evil Eye,* and Sir James George Frazer's study of traditional belief and myth, *The Golden Bough.*

In addition, I sincerely thank the Mediterranean villagers I met along the way, many of whom I never knew by name. They spontaneously and generously opened up their memories, hearts, and homes to share meals and stories of the colors known only to them.

Finally, I am eternally grateful to my wife, Sally Jean, for believing in me, for encouraging my travel even when it sometimes meant long periods apart, and for sharing so many of my journeys. Sally was my constant guide and working partner throughout the writing of the text and editing of the images for this book about the colors and places we both love.

For information regarding limited-edition photographs of images represented in this book, write Jeffrey Becom, Post Office Box 534, Pacific Grove, CA 93950-0534.

Select Bibliography

Allen, Edward. *Stone Shelters.* Cambridge: M.I.T. Press, 1969.

Ambasz, Emilio. *The Architecture of Luis Barragán.* New York: Museum of Modern Art, 1976.

Architectura popular em Portugal. Lisbon: National Union of Architects, 1961.

Athas, Daphne. *Greece by Prejudice.* Philadelphia: J. B. Lippincott, 1962.

Birren, Faber. *Color: A Survey in Words and Pictures from Ancient Mysticism to Modern Science.* Secaucus, New Jersey: Citadel Press, 1963.

Bogdanou-Eliopoulou, Maria, and Angeliki Fetokaki-Sarandidi. *Kalymnos.* Translated by Philip Ramp. Athens: "Melissa" Publishing House, 1984.

Boudier, Jean-Paul, and Trinh T. Minh-ha. *Africa Spaces: Designs for Living in Upper Volta.* New York: Africana/Holmes & Meier, 1985.

Bridge, Ann, and Susan Lowndes. *The Selective Traveller in Portugal.* New York: McGraw-Hill, 1967.

Carver, Norman F., Jr. *Iberian Villages: Portugal and Spain.* Kalamazoo, Michigan: Documan Press, 1981.

————. *Italian Hilltowns.* Kalamazoo, Michigan: Documan Press, 1979.

Coates, Robert M. *Beyond the Alps: A Summer in the Italian Hilltowns.* New York: William Sloane Associates, 1961.

Cornelisen, Ann. *Torregreca: Life, Death, Miracles.* New York: Delta, 1969.

Denyer, Susan. *African Traditional Architecture.* New York: Africana/Holmes & Meier, 1978.

Dicks, Brian. *Corfu.* London: David and Charles, 1977.

Ellingham, Mark, and Shaun McVeigh. *The Rough Guide to Morocco.* London: Routledge & Kegan Paul, 1985.

Elworthy, Frederick Thomas. *The Evil Eye: An Account of This Ancient and Widespread Superstition.* 1895; reprint ed., New York: Julian Press, 1986.

Etherton, P. T. *Across the Great Deserts.* New York: McGraw Hill, 1948.

Evans, Bill, and Andrew Lawson. *Shopfronts.* New York: Van Nostrand Reinhold, 1981.

Feduchi, Luis. *Spanish Folk Architecture.* Barcelona: Editorial Blume, 1982.

Frazer, Sir James George. *The Golden Bough: A Study of Magic and Religion.* New York: The Macmillan Company, 1922.

Fumagalli, Alberto. *The Peasant and His Home.* Translated by Yvonne Cassab. Milan: Calderini Edagricole, 1985.

Goldberger, Paul. *The City Observed.* New York: Random House, 1979.

Goldfinger, Myron. *Villages in the Sun: Mediterranean Community Architecture.* New York: Praeger Publishers, 1969.

Greek Traditional Architecture. Library of Art series, volumes 1–8. Athens: "Melissa" Publishing House, 1980– .

Heer, Friedrich, ed. *Milestones of History: The Fires of Faith.* New York: Newsweek Books, 1970.

Hersey, George. *The Lost Meaning of Classical Architecture: Speculations on Ornament from Vitruvius to Venturi* (Cambridge: M.I.T. Press, 1988).

Honour, Hugh. *The Companion Guide to Venice.* Englewood Cliffs, New Jersey: Prentice-Hall, 1965.

Keith, Agnes Newton. *Children of Allah.* New York: Atlantic Monthly Press, 1965.

Megas, George A. *The Greek House: Its Evolution and Its Relation to the Houses of Other Balkan Peoples.* New York: AMS Press, 1951.

Michener, James A. *Iberia.* New York: Random House, 1968.

Miller, Helen Hill. *Greek Horizons.* New York: Charles Scribner's Sons, 1961.

Moholy-Nagy, Dorothea Sibylle (Pietzsch). *Native Genius in Anonymous Architecture.* New York: Horizon Press, 1957.

Morton, H. V. *A Stranger in Spain.* New York: Dodd, Mead & Co., 1955.

———. *A Traveller in Italy.* New York: Dodd, Mead & Co., 1964.

———. *A Traveller in Southern Italy.* New York: Dodd, Mead & Co., 1969.

Oliver, Paul, ed. *Shelter, Sign and Symbol.* New York: Overlook Press, 1977.

Radice, Barbara. *Memphis: Research, Experiences, Results, Failures and Successes of New Design.* New York: Rizzoli International Publications, 1984.

Rapoport, Amos. *House, Form and Culture.* Englewood Cliffs, New Jersey: Prentice-Hall, 1969.

Riley, Noël. *Tile Art: A History of Decorative Ceramic Tiles.* Secaucus, New Jersey: Chartwell Books, 1987.

Riviére-Sestier, M. *Venice and the Islands.* Translated by Peter E. Thompson. New York: Pitman Publishing Corp., 1957.

Rudofsky, Bernard. *Architecture Without Architects.* New York: Museum of Modern Art, 1964.

Shimomura, J. *Meaning of Walls in Modern European Architecture.* Tokyo: Graphic-Sha/Books Nippan, 1984.

Simon, Kate. *Italy, the Places in Between.* New York: Harper & Row, 1970.

Simpson, Colin. *Europe, an Intimate View.* New York: A. S. Barnes, 1960.

Sitwell, Sacheverell. *Portugal and Madeira.* London: B. T. Batsford, 1954.

Slesin, Suzanne, Stafford Cliff, and Daniel Rozensztroch. *Greek Style.* New York: Clarkson N. Potter, 1988.

Starkie, Walter. *The Road to Santiago: Pilgrims of St. James.* Berkeley: University of California Press, 1957.

Stern, Robert A.M., with Raymond W. Gastil. *Modern Classicism.* New York: Rizzoli International, 1988.

Symons, Arthur. *Cities of Italy.* New York: E. P. Dutton & Co., 1907.

Vakirtzis, Giorgos, Panayotis Gravalos, and Kostas Tzimoulis. *Greek Shop Signs.* Athens: Papastratos Company, 1980.

Varley, Helen, ed. *Colour.* London: Marshall Editions, 1983.

Vegas, Federico. *Venezuelan Vernacular.* New York: Princeton Architectural Press, 1985.

Vidal, Gore, and George Armstrong. *Vidal in Venice.* New York: Summit Books, 1985.

Whelpton, Eric and Barbara. *Greece & the Islands.* New York: Roy Publishers, 1961.

Index

Editor: Alan Axelrod
Designer: James Wageman
Production supervisor: Hope Koturo

First edition
10 9 8 7 6

Library of Congress Cataloging-in-Publication Data
Becom, Jeffrey.
  Mediterranean color / photographs and text by Jeffrey Becom; foreword by Paul Goldberger.
    p. cm.
  Includes bibliographical references.
  ISBN 0-89659-925-6
  1. Vernacular architecture—Mediterranean Region. I. Title.
NA1458.B4 1990   89-18063
779'.41822—dc20

Jacket front: Yellow Wall, Pisa, Italy
Jacket background and back: Shuttered Door, Gallipoli, Italy
Half-title page: Torn Poster, Florence, Italy
Frontispiece: Blue Steps, Kalymnos, Greece
Page 4: Cane Chair, Burano, Italy
Contents page: Red Chimney, Burano, Italy

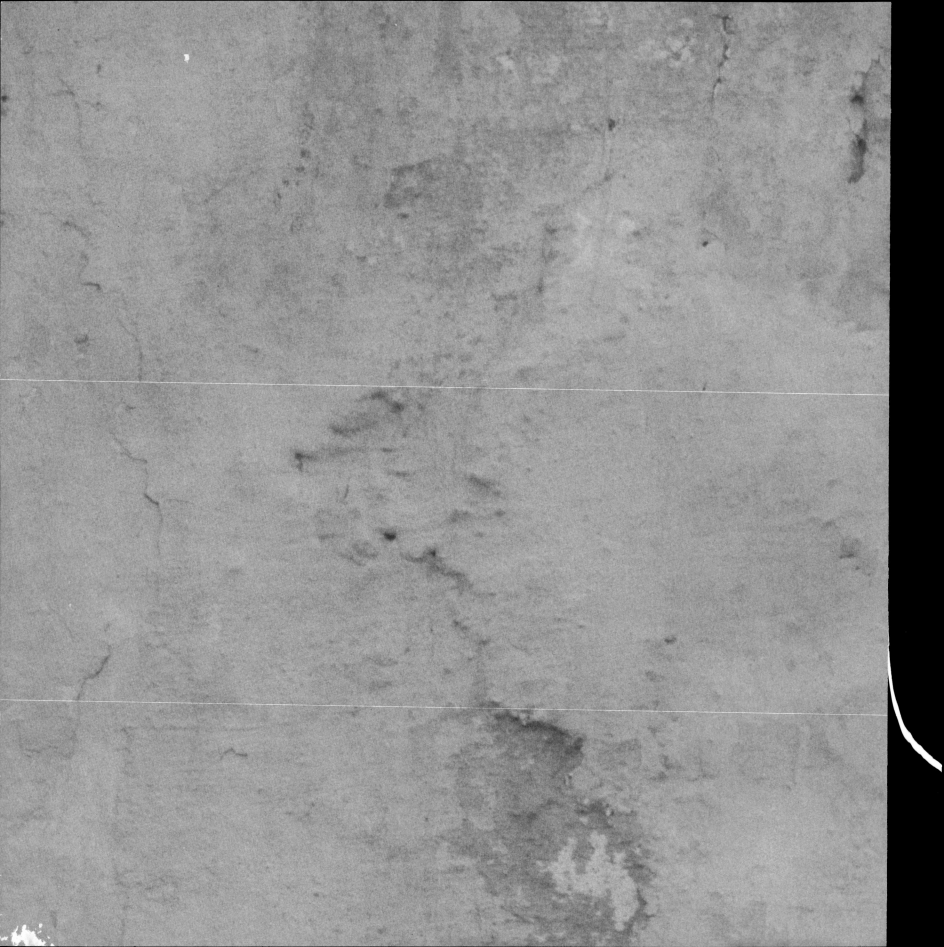